MICHAEL MOORER

# KINGDOM

## — M E N —

GOD'S MIND ON THE MATTER

Copyright © 2023 Michael Moorer
www.michaelmoorerbooks.com
Social media: @michaelmoorerbooks
Book cover design: Jared Michael |
Instagram.com/jaredmichaeldesignco
Book editors: Michael Moorer, Travis Eades & Melson Tookes
Book formatting: Melson Tookes | goshenconsultingmd.com
Photography: Andrae Jiles / Michael Moorer Photography

ISBN: 979-8395311276

# Table of Contents

# Acknowledgements

I am incredibly grateful to God for life and the privilege to worship Him in spirit and truth. I'm beyond grateful to be chosen for such a time as this. My life didn't make sense to me for a long time until I fully surrendered all of myself to the Lord. He then opened my eyes and revealed whom He called me to be. God's faithfulness has forever changed me! I wouldn't trade Him in for the world or no material possession! I'm still awed by the Lord's grace enabling me to write my eighth book. I appreciate having a fantastic team to help me complete this book assignment from the Lord, "Kingdom Men," with excellence and integrity.

**Melson Tookes**, thank you for all your consistent sacrifices and support. If only the world knew how much of a right-hand man you are to me and the many things you assist me with, they would be beyond amazed! You are a class act, my friend! Thank you so much for everything! I love and appreciate you enormously! May the Lord prosper and make everything you do tremendously successful. You more than deserve it! May the favor of God flood your life until Jesus returns! **Travis Eades**, your consistency, kindness, friendship, and service is always great! You are one of the most selfless individuals I know. I've watched you grow by leaps and bounds for many years, and you are not average because you have depth and embrace the hard truth. I pray that God continues to shift your life to realms of glory that will make you shake your head in awe. Thank you for always sowing your priceless time editing my books and your money into buying them afterward.

**Apostle Dion Nesmith**, you've been more to me than you know. You have been the best spiritual father and mentor a man could ask for. Since 2016 up to this very moment, your impact on my life has been mind-blowing. I respect and honor you for all you do and the time you continue to invest in me. I genuinely love you, your wife (Prophetess Janice L. Nesmith), and the VOTD family! You will always be a part of my godly legacy in the Earth and Heaven. Thank you for receiving me during a vulnerable time and transition in my life. I pray God gives you and Prophetess Janice a golden crown encrusted with thousands of precious diamonds with uncalculatable carats. You and your family are special jewels to the world at large and especially to the body of Christ. May your cups never run dry but remain in a place of overflow. **John and Clara Moorer (my lovely parents)**, thank you for everything! I honor and love you both. You all gave me the most incredible legacy of all times, the Word of God—Jesus! Because of your consistency in ensuring my siblings and I had a foundation in Christ when we couldn't defend ourselves, you can now see the fruit of your labor in the land of the living. I pray that you both have front-row seats in Heaven. There are so many things I can say thank you for, but it will turn into another book. Many people wish they had parents who raised them with the standards of the Lord. I'm grateful I didn't have to wish. I am who I am and whom I'm becoming because of both your prayers, parenting, and the impartation of God's Word into my life. Thank you for being an example, and I pray that God will continue to cause both your prayers and desires to manifest now and eternally.

**Jared Michael**, you always deliver! Thank you for consistently birthing my vision when I ask you to design my newest book cover. You've outdone yourself with this design, and I want the world to know I love it! I pray the Lord continues to bless your business and give you fresh artistic expressions and designs that you or anyone else have yet to see worldwide! May your eyes and hands prophetically see and create from the throne of God! Lastly, **Andrae Jiles**, thank you for capturing my awesome photos for this book. I gave you a challenge, and you survived well! You have a great eye! Also, your work ethic and your gift of hospitality are second to none! Thank you for always stepping in and getting the job done whenever I need you! Congratulations on your first book cover and published photography—Kingdom Men!

# Introduction

Looking at where most men are today, we can see that a fierce enemy attack has been launched against us, whether believers or unbelievers. To win this vicious spiritual war, we must know who we are in Christ and who the Lord called us to be as kingdom ambassadors (people who represent God) versus mere religious men maintaining a form of godliness that lacks true power and authority. Everything men are missing in their identity is in Jesus—The Word. To unlock God's purpose for our lives, we must first become students of His Word. Truthfully, the totality of our issues as men is a lack of intimacy and obedience to the Father. Once we develop a real relationship with God and abort the carnal worldview of manhood, we will transition out of religion, pride, and hard-heartedness and into His original intent.

The Word of the Lord is our standard and manual for kingdom living, no matter the subject or issue. Colossians 3:2 KJV tells us to *"Set your affection on things above, not on the things on the earth."* Colossians confirms that our focus and affection should be on pleasing the Lord. As godly men, we're to live from Heaven to Earth and not Earth to Heaven, confirming that our position as men is to seek the Lord above everything and everyone. When we pursue the Kingdom of God, we pursue Yahweh (God) because He is the Kingdom!

*"But first and most importantly seek (aim at, strive after) His kingdom and His righteousness [His way of doing and being right—the attitude and character of God], and all these things will be given to you also." Matthew 6:33 AMP*

Kingdom men are ambassadors of Jesus Christ. What is an ambassador? An ambassador is a well-equipped individual sent out by an official governing figure as a representative of him or her, a foreign country, a group of people, or a brand. Since God is the governing King in our lives as believers, we're supposed to represent Him in everything we do. We must live our daily lives as if we're already in Heaven because Jesus is the same yesterday, today, and forever (see Hebrews 13:8). God's standards are eternal! Kingdom men stick with God and His Word because He's the only Sovereign Governor from whom we take our orders. To take our rightful place in the Earth as men of God, we must fully surrender to the Lord and worship only Him. Adam's manhood started by being in the presence of the Lord when He created him from the dust of the ground. The moment God created Adam and blew the breath of life in Him (see Genesis 2:7), Adam was in the presence of the Father, the Son (Jesus, who is the Word), and the Holy Spirit. How do I know? Because God said, *"Let us make man in our image (see Genesis 1:26)."* The Father, Son, and the Holy Spirit are one. The most important place we can ever live in is the presence of God.

God's men (and women) are royal priests, a chosen people, a holy nation, and His possession. We are people called out of darkness and into God's marvelous light. If we truly belong to the Lord (by being born again through Jesus Christ), we must represent Him in our spirit, soul, and body. We must also live holy and righteous lives that please the Lord. We are men of the light and not of the dark! *Kingdom Men* challenges what we've been taught and believed in for many years with the standards of the Word. The truth will always be a racking ball that dismantles deception, misinformation, and error. So let's prepare our hearts and minds to shift from what we thought was true about manhood to what is biblically sound. This book has the power (because it's full of the Word) to remove the invisible grave clothes of religion and lifeless traditions from us and replace them with God's invisible priestly garments. In addition, the teachings in this book will cause us to take our eyes off other men so that we can become the men God created us to be. Remember, God's way is the best way to live because any other way is incorrect. I decree and declare each man who reads this book will experience true deliverance and freedom from falsehood, the demonic indoctrinations of the world, and ungodly practices. It's time for men to become kingdom citizens of Yahweh and His version of a man. Lastly, authentic manhood was established by Elohim (the God of all creation) through Jesus and carried out in the Earth as the Ultimate and Divine

Prototype for kingdom men. Welcome to Kingdom Men: God's Mind on the Matter!

# CHAPTER ONE

# Identity Crisis

We live in a world where we look to others for an identity when we don't know who we are in Christ. But when we know who the Lord called us to be, we pursue His original intent (who we're supposed to be in the Earth for the Father) and not a man-made concept or standard. The prototype for all of humanity is Jesus! Unfortunately, every person will not become a born-again biblical believer. But Jesus is always ready to receive any who is willing to change (repent) their life and receive Him as their Lord and Savior. As kingdom men of God, it is essential for us to know we are called to be like Jesus Christ. He is the one we're supposed to admire and look to for an understanding of how to function as confident kingdom men. We can't physically look at Jesus, but His Word gives us everything we need to live and carry out our manhood according to God's original design.

Contrary to popular belief, there are no two men who are completely alike. We have similarities because we are men, but we are different by the intentional design of God. Our upbringing and life experiences also add to our differences even though we are men. However, if we want to know if we're in alignment with who God called and created us to be, it starts and continues with His Word. Many people view the word "identity crisis" as someone who is confused about their sexuality but that is not always the case. That's a part of it but not the totality of an identity crisis. There are many men who are sure about their sexuality but clueless about the man God called them to be. This too is an issue of identity. Nevertheless, before we understand who we truly are we must have an intimate relationship with the Lord through His Word (Jesus). Since many men don't have a personal relationship with the Lord, they categorize (group, grade, label) themselves with other men (and sometimes women) not realizing that each man is created to be uniquely different by God. So we end up becoming a counterfeit version of someone else because they look like what we think we should be. When we're unaware of who we are in Christ, we measure ourselves amongst our peers. We literally mimic who they are (as well as covet what they have) as if they are the standard. Whenever we measure ourselves amongst ourselves, we dishonor God, His Word, and ourselves.

*"Oh, don't worry; we wouldn't dare say that we are as wonderful as these other men who tell you how important they are! But they are only comparing themselves with each other, using themselves as the standard of measurement. How ignorant!" 2 Corinthians 10:12 NLT*

It's okay for men to be inspired by other men. However, we shouldn't lose who we are because it appears that someone else knows how to be a better man than our example—Jesus. That will never be the case! Jesus is forever the greatest man (who was fully human and divine) who ever walked the earth! Being a man is not about mimicking another man who appears to have it all together. But it is about being a godly man who operates as a king and priest in the earth. From a biblical and foundational perspective, kings had influence over the people and the priests had direct access to God. Still today, the Lord wants us to be men of His Word who walks in close fellowship (relationship) with Him daily. He also wants us to carry godly influence in the Earth so we can win souls to Christ and show unbelievers how a real man is supposed to carry himself in public, at home, in the marketplace, and in the house of the Lord. Even though people can't see who we are behind closed doors, God can, and He matters more than anyone! Plus, who we are when no one else can see us eventually becomes public information whether good or bad. Selah! What's done in the dark is always exposed by the light.

*"For nothing is secret that will not be revealed, nor anything hidden that will not be known and come to light."* Luke 8:17 NKJV

When our manhood (maturity, masculinity) is aligned with the Word of God, our choices in life birth good fruit. When our manhood is aligned with the Word of God, we won't get entangled with ungodly women or intentionally operate outside of our covenant with the Lord. In addition, when our manhood is aligned with the Word of God, we will marry one woman and remain faithful to her throughout the marriage. When it comes to the children, godly men (who are aligned with the Word) train and raise up their children in godliness so that the satanic systems of the world won't raise them. Their children have a foundation of truth (the Word) that gives them the ability to discern good from evil. On the contrary, if we are single men we must live according to the Word of God as well. Our single status doesn't exempt us from walking in full faithfulness to the Lord publicly and privately. We must remain focused and place our time and energy solely on what God has purposed us to do. So that when it's time to get married, we know who we are as well as our divine purpose from God. Nevertheless, if a single man chooses not to marry, then his whole life is to remain totally devoted to the Lord because he doesn't have a wife to share his life with. The Word confirms an unmarried man should spend his time pleasing the Lord and doing His work in the Earth (see 1 Corinthians 1:32-34).

Moreover, being faithful to a ministry leader or attending church is not the same as being in a loyal and intimate relationship with the Lord. Serving in the house of the Lord is essential! But that doesn't replace the close relationship we should have with the Lord. We can work for God without ever knowing Him personally due to a lack of consistent fellowship. Most saved men have a second-hand relationship with the Lord. What do I mean? A second-hand relationship with God is when we know Him through someone else, but we haven't had a personal encounter of our own to validate what we know. Once we become old enough to understand who the Lord is and the importance of daily communion with Him, we are responsible for our own spiritual work and soul salvation. If we want to be true men of God, we must be able to access the Lord personally through His Word, prayer, fasting, and worship (which is the totality of a surrendered life to Him). The only way we can solve our identity crisis is by submitting to Yahweh, the one who gave and continues to give us life daily, divine purpose in the earth, and our identity. There's no other way around it! Here's the confirmation of who we are (our identity): *"But you are a chosen race, a royal priesthood, a dedicated nation, [God's] own purchased, special people, that you may set forth the wonderful deeds and display the virtues and perfections of Him Who called you out of darkness into His marvelous light. 1 Peter 2:9 AMPC*

To drive this point home, we must settle this truth in our hearts and minds that we are not called to be like the next man. We are called to be like Christ! The Spirit of the Lord says, *"Since many of us do a great job at copying other men (who are mere humans), we shouldn't have any problem with copying Jesus, who was the ultimate example of a kingdom man who completed the will of the Father."* If we get lost in being like Christ, we'll be found in right standing with God. But if we get lost in being a false representative of someone else, we will live unfulfilled, incomplete, and out of alignment with the Lord. We will also continue to search outwardly to find in something or someone that can ONLY be found in Jesus alone! It's in Him we find our identity!

**Scripture references:**

- *For in Him we live and move and have our being; as even some of your [own] poets have said, for we are also His offspring. Acts 17:28 AMPC*

- *Therefore be imitators of God [copy Him and follow His example], as well-beloved children [imitate their father]. Ephesians 5:1 AMPC*

# Signs of an Identity Crisis

One of the ways to know if we have an identity crisis is by looking to see if we've become like the individuals that inspire us or an image of the current culture. Most men (and humanity) are highly seduced by what they hear and see daily. Instead of taking a moment to think critically for themselves, they automatically believe everything their favorite influencers (musical artists, actors, ministry leaders, etc.) present them with (in words or deeds) because they have become their image and voice of truth instead of the Word. From a cultural perspective, what we see, hear, and place a high value on causes us to question our worth and value because we're different from what the world model before us. What we see as successful, prosperous, happy, and the like are mostly smoke and mirrors. But we won't know until God awaken us to the truth. Male influencers disciple numerous amounts of men who are trying to find themselves through them. They are copying what they consistently see without realizing their celebrity role model, church leader, friend, rapper, singer, and the like have an identity crisis too! In other words, the lost are mimicking the lost! But when we find Christ for real, we go from lost to found. Let's be clear about one thing; we can be a leader in a church and still suffer from identity issues. A life in Christ validates our identity, but merely working in and attending church (without having a loyal relationship to the Lord through obeying all His Word) doesn't. I had to clarify that because ministry leaders can also mislead us! Some ministry leaders are not suitable to follow or be inspired by. Therefore, knowing God and His Word is essential for understanding who we are and the difference between good and evil. When we wear deception (the identity of someone or something else), we waste time being a counterfeit instead maximizing our time being God's original intent. We must confront and abort our identity crisis so that who we are in Christ can be made manifest in and through us.

**Here's a list that reveals manifestations of an identity crisis:**

1. When we're searching outside of Jesus for spiritual fulfillment
2. Your life mimics others you're inspired by
3. When we hang out with the wrong crowd for acceptance and validation
4. When our appearance matches our favorite artist
5. We look for love in all the wrong places
6. When we're clueless about who God called us to be
7. Unaware of our purpose
8. Not feeling a sense of purpose or understating your value in Christ
9. Insecurity
10. We fit in with the cultures of the world
11. Self-comparison
12. When we live the world's version of a man and not God's version (Jesus)
13. Feeling unwanted
14. Always quoting what others say as if it's the truth
15. When a perverted lifestyle becomes our usual way of living
16. People pleaser
17. When we remain in the same place because it nurtures our familiarity
18. When we lack the courage to be an individual
19. Abandonment

20. When we're loyal to handed-down traditions but unfaithful to God
21. When sexual promiscuity validates our manhood
22. Consistently switching out dating partners
23. When we gain confidence and comfort from social media likes and comments
24. When we're impressed by celebrities
25. Inferior (when we feel less than the next person or someone we admire)
26. When we worship and depend on the creations of God but not Him (crystals, the universe, sun worship, etc.)
27. Worth and value gained by money and materialistic things
28. Jealousy
29. Homosexuality (a perverse spiritual stronghold that creates an identity crisis inwardly that manifests outwardly)
30. Depression

This list of thirty items isn't written for unbelievers but for believers. However, this checklist and book will be essential when ungodly men are ready to give their life to Christ. Some men faithfully attend the house of the Lord, work in ministry, and even shepherd a local church that deals with many of the issues listed. How is this so? A lack of knowledge (see Hosea 4:6) and operating from a religious mindset instead of an intimate relationship with the Lord. Once we shift from lifeless religious practices (where we constantly rehearse the traditions of man) to walking in the kingdom and biblical understanding, we will walk away from everything that doesn't represent God and His original intent concerning us and His will. The Lord is the only one who can free us from our identity crisis and restore our original intent in Him. The more we truly know the Lord, the more our life becomes about pleasing Him and completing everything He has placed in our hands. Living in Christ dismantles all false identities so that our royal identity becomes who we are in Christ. Men of God, we are kings and priests with tailor-made destinies from the Lord. Be free from your identity crisis so that the Lord can fill every void lingering in you.

# CHAPTER TWO

# Kingdom Order

Everything about God's kingdom has rank and order. So does the kingdom of Satan because he copied the system and structure of the Lord and formed perverse versions of his own. Satan knows how Heaven operates because he once resided there. If we plan to be kingdom men who don't operate from a perverted nature, we must do things God's way. In Yahweh's kingdom, things only go His way! Since God is the Creator of everyone and everything, He calls the shots without having to get them approved. Also, there's no democracy (a system based on the people's votes) in the kingdom of God; only His Word, culture, and standards are allowed. Therefore, to be authentic worshippers of the Lord, He must be first place in our lives. Kingdom Men, we can't live successful single or married lives without God as number one. Worldly success and Godly success are entirely different. We can be millionaires in the Earth and bankrupt in the Lord and Heaven. If we're not living according to the will of the Father, we're automatically living according to our own. We can't be self-centered without being rebellious because we must rebel against God's will to accomplish our own. However, obedience to God and His Word equals success now and even more on the day of judgment. What we need to know about rebellion is that it is as the sin of witchcraft (see 1 Samuel 15:24). As kingdom men, we take orders from the King of Glory (Yahweh) and not the King of Darkness (Satan).

Adam was the first kingdom man created. The Lord placed him in the Garden of Eden to tend, guard, and keep it (see Genesis 2:15). This reveals that Adam had his assignment from God before a wife was needed and created for him. While Adam worked in the garden, the Lord said, "it wasn't good for him to be alone." So He made Adam a suitable and complementary helpmeet (wife) and called her Eve (see Genesis 2:22). This prophetically reveals that Adam was already a husband before becoming one. Selah! It also shows that the Most High God (Yahweh) created marriage. Marriage is a spiritual and sacred covenant that represents His church as the bride of Christ. On the contrary, when a man and woman live together unmarried, that is an ungodly practice that imitates marriage. In addition, it is an unlawful union the Lord will not approve or bless. God doesn't bless sin of any sort, but Satan sure does! Demonic spirits influence and inhabit (dwell, live, abides) our sins because they fit within the confines of Satan's covenant which results in death and destruction (unless we repent and live according to God's will and design). Before Adam ate the forbidden fruit (Yahweh instructed him not to do so in Genesis 2: 16-17), he was in worship unto God, which means he was entirely in His will. True worship is a life surrendered (spirit, soul, and body) to the King of Glory! For clarity, worship is not a slow or fast song. Music, in general, is not worship. Music is an art and heart of expression created with one or more sounds from different instruments. In addition, music is a spiritual tool that assists us with our inward and outward expression of adoration and love towards God or Satan. Nonetheless, we automatically yield to Satan when we don't submit to the Lord. There are no in-between options! God created All creation to worship Him. We were made by Him (God) and for Him. The Lord also designed us to house His Spirit. But we are not willing to offer our lives to the Lord, our worship automatically goes to something or someone because God created us to worship Him only. I will cover more about worship in depth in another chapter.

Maintaining divine order is essential to stay within the confines of God's structure (order). Our lives are protected from Satan when we remain in God's will and Word. It is also imperative for us to know our purpose in life by seeking first His kingdom (God), and all things will be added unto us (see

Matthew 6:33). The Lord must always be our number one priority before anything or anyone (married or single). Because anything or anyone that comes before the Father is a false god we have erected in our lives. Kingdom order starts with God first! When we keep God as our primary source as men, He keeps us satisfied, peaceful, and strengthened for every task ahead. He makes sure we have everything we need. Once we get married, the wife comes in second place and the children third. Here's biblical and prophetic confirmation: Yahweh has always existed. He created Adam followed by Eve (his wife) and later their children (Cain and Able). The order of God is EVERYTHING! If we want to live in synergy with the Creator, we must live within the confines of His Word and order.

# A Breach of Kingdom Order

Now that we understand kingdom order and the importance of keeping God first, it's time to expose one of the breaches in God's structure for families causing global dysfunction. Men are essential pillars of their families and the world at large. What are a few synonyms for the word "pillar?" Support, backbone, and foundation. As men, we are responsible for being the backbone of our wives and children. We are solid backbones for them when we make God our backbone by abiding in His Word. When we lean on God as our Divine Pillar, we can extend that power to our family and beyond. However, apart from God, we can do nothing acceptable to Him! Our job is to maintain the Lord's perfect will (instead of His permissive will) and structure because they yield His righteous results. *"Yes, I am the vine; you are the branches. Those who remain in me, and I in them, will produce much fruit. For apart from me you can do nothing." John 15:5 NLT*

Men called to be single are supposed to devote their whole life to God, including the vocation and ministry work He called to them. Men who are single but desire to be married should keep God first in everything, prepare themselves for their wives, and maintain spiritual, mental, and physical purity (holiness). If they mess up on their purity (holiness) journey, repent (change and turn back to God) and keep doing things the Lord's way. On the other hand, married men must keep their relationship with God first and spend time with their spouse to ensure her needs and well-being. In other words, married men must please and be faithful to God and their wives. The interests and concerns of husbands are between the Lord and their spouses (and children, if they have any). I keep putting "God first" to remind us that anything that takes His place becomes an idol god. Wives are our help meets but not our Sovereign King! Selah!

One of the most significant issues in our homes is the lack of husbands and wives that disciple their children with the Word of God. Since men are the leaders of their homes, they're supposed to partner with their wives in making godly disciples out of their children before the world corrupts them. Due to broken marriages, fatherless homes, and believers who carry a form of godliness, the enemy has become the influencer of the family. So instead of the parents influencing their children with the mind of Christ (the Word), they indoctrinate them with the world's ways through their actions and lifestyle. On the contrary, women can raise godly children without men, but God's original intent is for husbands and wives to do that work together.

Moreover, Satan knows when the pillar of the home is removed from its structure because it becomes less supported. The lack of structural support from the pillar (the man of the house) causes the backbone of the family structure to weaken until it completely collapses. When men aren't the pillars of their homes, they undermine the family structure and create open doors for the enemy to gain access to their wives and children. This truth doesn't solely apply to men missing from their homes altogether. It also applies to men who are in their homes but spiritually and emotionally absent in their relationship with God and their families.

In closing, it's not God's intent for wives to solely be prayer warriors, disciplines, teachers, etc. As men of God, we should always be the headliners in our homes to ensure we are godly examples to our wives and children. We are not good fathers and husbands (what the Lord considers good) if we don't have a relationship with the King of Glory (the Father). In addition, we can't be in proper authority if we are not living under God's authority. Men of God, the Lord wants quality time and intimacy with each of us because it is a part of true worship offered to Him. It is also a part of godly leadership. We can fix the breach in our homes by repairing our relationship with the Lord, which causes everything else to fall in divine alignment.

# Hidden Jealousy

Many male ministry leaders and husbands in the body of Christ are against women ministry leaders. Some guys are against women in leadership, even within the world's systems. Many men do all they can to keep women (especially their wives) from being all of whom God called them to be. It's mainly because of biblical teachings taken out of context, jealousy, and incompetence. Kingdom men are not jealous of women in ministry, their wives, or the women they are preparing to marry (those who are single). Why is this? Because they understand God is no respecter of persons and that He uses women to do many wondrous works in the body of Christ and the marketplace as He does men. When it comes to marriages, women are indeed their husbands' helpmeet (a helpful companion). It's biblical! But women are not the slave (manservants, laborers, captives) of their husbands. Helpmeet and enslaved person are two different terms. Genesis 2:18 AMPC says, *"Now the Lord God said, it is not good (sufficient, satisfactory) that the man should be alone; I will make him a helper meet (suitable, adapted, complementary) for him."* One of the reasons God created women is to help manifest the vision God gave their husbands. Women are natural multipliers. If men don't have a vision for where God is taking them, they don't need to seek out a wife just yet because they don't have anything to multiply. Instead, the seek should be after God and the assignment He has for them. Knowing and perusing your God-given call is even more important than having a wife. Selah! Women need men who have their work and understand their call, as Adam did before the Lord made him a wife (helpmeet).

God did not create women so that they could be slaves to their husband's pride and insecurities. Our responsibility as men is to get delivered from pride and insecurity because those are two areas of strongholds that need to break. In addition, women have a purpose beyond being mere wives or single women waiting to be married. God calls them into the business world, the five-fold ministry offices, government, etc. A kingdom woman knows how to simultaneously be a godly wife, mover and shaker (powerful and influential), entrepreneur, and the like in the earth. The Lord didn't give women gifts and callings to go unused just because we're insecure as men. Women don't need to possess the Holy Spirit if their only job from God is to have sex with their husbands, wash dishes, and clean the home. Many unsaved women are doing these things well without the Holy Spirit! The areas mentioned are essential within a marriage and family; however, they are not the totality of most (if not all) women's lives and purposes. In essence, there is more to kingdom women than the box most men and husbands keep them in due to jealousy, insecurity, wrong teachings, and bad influences.

A godly woman knows how to be submissive to her husband at home and a boss at work without confusing the two. If she knows who she is in Christ and her role as a wife, things will flow according to God's Word. When we are submitted to God first and foremost, everything else falls in line. Most men want women to submit to them while they submit to no one. The correct order for kingdom men is to stay submitted and committed to God while their wives are submitted and committed to them. This order doesn't mean women shouldn't have their relationship with the Lord because He's also first in their lives. Women are not to worship their husbands, and husbands are not to worship their wives to avoid idolatry. Men and women have access to the Father— Yahweh through the Son—Jesus. If men want to be who they're supposed to be to their wives and children, they must submit to God. A husband can't lead his wife and family in the right direction unless He's allowing God to lead him first. As I mentioned, true headship occurs when men are in personal communion with the Lord and under His authority. Authority begets authority! Honestly, if it weren't for women doing the work of God, many lives would still be lost. God needs "All hands on deck" to accomplish His will in the Earth and not just the hands of men (males). Countless men don't want to do their jobs in many areas or want anyone else to do them. God doesn't support this chauvinist, envious, and religious spirit toward women. The Lord will use anyone He pleases to accomplish His will in the earth. He's Sovereign!

*"And it shall come to pass in the last days, God declares, that I will pour out of My Spirit upon all mankind, and your sons and your daughters shall prophesy [telling forth the divine counsels] and your young men shall see visions (divinely granted appearances), and your old men shall dream [divinely suggested] dreams." Acts 2:17 AMPC*

When Jesus ascended back to Heaven, He left ministerial offices (gifts), and none of them came with genitalia. Selah! Therefore, the gifts of Jesus aren't released gender specific. Once again, God is Sovereign! He can do and use whomever

He wants! Truthfully, if more men would step up to the plate and be who God called us to be, the women of God wouldn't have to work as hard. The scales would be well balanced. Nevertheless, the Lord uses who and what is available to accomplish His mission. Women are more available to God and His will than men due to their lack of intimacy and surrender to Him.

**Here's our scriptural confirmation:**

*"(Now this expression, "He ascended," what does it mean except that He also had previously descended [from the heights of heaven] into the lower parts of the earth? He who descended is the very same as He who also has ascended high above all the heavens, that He [His presence] might fill all things [that is, the whole universe]). And [His gifts to the church were varied and] He Himself appointed some as apostles [special messengers, representatives], some as prophets [who speak a new message from God to the people], some as evangelists [who spread the good news of salvation], and some as pastors and teachers [to shepherd and guide and instruct], [and He did this] to fully equip and perfect the saints (God's people) for works of service, to build up the body of Christ [the church]; until we all reach oneness in the faith and in the knowledge of the Son of God, [growing spiritually] to become a mature believer, reaching to the measure of the fullness of Christ [manifesting His spiritual completeness and exercising our spiritual gifts in unity]. So that we are no longer children [spiritually immature], tossed back and forth [like ships on a stormy sea] and carried about by every wind of [shifting] doctrine, by the cunning and trickery of [unscrupulous] men, by the deceitful scheming of people ready to do anything [for personal profit]." Ephesians 4:9-14 AMP*

Women are incredibly vital to the world. But some men will not acknowledge this truth because of their ego (arrogance, pride, narcissism). A man with the spirit of pride will never admit when he's wrong to his wife or women in general. We must remove pride from our lives because pride is the same spirit that got Satan kicked out of Heaven. Yet, pride will be why so many men won't make it to Heaven (see Isaiah 14:12-15 and Ezekiel 28: 12-15) unless they repent and develop an authentic relationship with the Lord through Jesus Christ. Men of God, it's time that we allow the Lord to recalibrate our minds to the truth of His Word (in place of our egos), so we can have the mind of Christ.

**Scripture references:**

- *Be subject to one another out of reverence for Christ (the Messiah, the Anointed One). Wives, be subject (be submissive and adapt yourselves) to your own husbands as [a service] to the Lord. For the husband is head of the wife as Christ is the Head of the church, Himself the Savior of [His] body. As the church is subject to Christ, so let wives also be subject in everything to their husbands. Husbands, love your wives, as Christ loved the church and gave Himself up for her, so that He might sanctify her, having cleansed her by the washing of water with the Word, That He might present the church to Himself in glorious splendor, without spot or wrinkle or any such things [that she might be holy and faultless]. Even so husbands should love their wives as [being in a sense] their own bodies. He who loves his own wife loves himself. For no man ever hated his own flesh, but nourishes and carefully protects and cherishes it, as Christ does the church." Ephesians 5:21-29 AMPC*

- *In the same way, you husbands must give honor to your wives. Treat your wife with understanding as you live together. She may be weaker than you are, but she is your equal partner in God's gift of new life. Treat her as you should so your prayers will not be hindered. 1 Peter 3:7 NLT*

Lastly, the Proverbs 31 woman is an excellent example of a kingdom woman with a husband who loved and respected her. She also had children and a productive life that yielded great fruit. She didn't neglect her responsibilities as a wife, yet she operated her day-to-day life with wisdom and precision. Just because a godly woman is productive and purpose-driven doesn't mean she's a woman exerting authority over her husband. When men and women genuinely revere and love the Lord according to His Word, both parties will know their roles and walk in them successfully. However, trouble and civil war are inevitable when one or two parties live out of synch with God and His Word! God warns us not to be unequally yoked with unbelievers for these reasons. Being unequally yoked means not aligning or marrying someone who is spiritually immature or out of covenant with Christ (an unbeliever or a professed believer who lives like an unbeliever). I can't stress this enough, men who don't have a relationship with the Lord do not lead according to God's intent. Outstanding leadership starts and remains with being in close fellowship with the Lord and His Word (which includes walking in the Holy Spirit). We can't expect women to follow us when we refuse to follow God. As mentioned, the divine protocol for godly men is for them to lead their families with the instructions and standards of the Lord. Everything outside of this order is disorder! To whom much is given, much is required! Titles and roles come with real responsibilities!

**Scripture references:**

- *All who fear the Lord will hate evil. Therefore, I hate pride and arrogance, corruption and perverse speech. Proverbs 8:13 NLT*

- *Pride goes before destruction, and haughtiness before a fall. Proverbs 16:18 NLT*

- *But He gives us more and more grace (power of the Holy Spirit, to meet this evil tendency and all others fully). That is why He says, God sets Himself against the proud and haughty, but gives grace [continually] to the lowly (those who are humble enough to receive it). James 4:6 AMPC*

- *Not everyone who says to Me, Lord, Lord, will enter the kingdom of heaven, but he who does the will of My Father Who is in heaven. Many will say to Me on that day, Lord, Lord, have we not prophesied in Your name and driven out demons in Your name and done many mighty works in Your name? And then I will say to them openly (publicly), I never knew you; depart from Me, you who act wickedly [disregarding My commands]. Matthew 7:21-23 AMPC*

Here are a few scripture references (but not limited to what's listed) of Women being used in leadership by God and how He's going to pour out His Spirit on all humanity in the last days which we are in:

1. Phoebe was a deacon (servant) in the Church in Cenchrea.

   Priscilla and Aquila worked in the ministry of Christ Jesus. They also showed Apollos (a man who was well-educated, cultured, and eloquent) a more excellent way.

   - *I commend to you our sister Phoebe, who is a deacon in the church in Cenchrea. Welcome her in the Lord as one who is worthy of honor among*

*God's people. Help her in whatever she needs, for she has been helpful to many, and especially to me. Give my greetings to Priscilla and Aquila, my co-workers in the ministry of Christ Jesus. In fact, they once risked their lives for me. I am thankful to them, and so are all the Gentile churches. Romans 16:1-4 NLT*

- *Meanwhile, there was a Jew named Apollos, a native of Alexandria, who came to Ephesus. He was a cultured and eloquent man, well versed and mighty in the Scriptures. He had been instructed in the way of the Lord, and burning with spiritual zeal, he spoke and taught diligently and accurately the things concerning Jesus, though he was acquainted only with the baptism of John. He began to speak freely (fearlessly and boldly) in the synagogue; but when Priscilla and Aquila heard him, they took him with them and expounded to him the way of God more definitely and accurately. Acts 18:24-26 AMPC*

2. Deborah was a judge over all of Israel who led and gave instructions to men. She was also a prophetess.

- *But after Ehud died the Israelites again did evil in the sight of the Lord. So the Lord sold them into the hand of Jabin king of Canaan, who reigned in Hazor. The commander of his army was Sisera, who dwelt in Harosheth-hagoiim [fortress or city of the nations]. Then the Israelites cried to the Lord, for [Jabin] had 900 chariots of iron and had severely oppressed the Israelites for twenty years. Now Deborah, a prophetess, the wife of Lappidoth, judged Israel at that time. She sat under the palm tree of Deborah between Ramah and Bethel in the hill country of Ephraim, and the Israelites came up to her for judgment. And she sent and called Barak son of Abinoam from Kedesh in Naphtali and said to him, Has not the Lord, the God of Israel, commanded [you], Go, gather your men at Mount Tabor, taking 10,000 men from the tribes of Naphtali and Zebulun? And I will draw out Sisera, the general of Jabin's army, to meet you at the river Kishon with his chariots and his multitude, and I will deliver him into your hand? And Barak said to her, If you will go with me, then I will go; but if you will not go with me, I will not go. And she said, I will surely go with you; nevertheless, the trip you take will not be for your glory, for the Lord will sell Sisera into the hand of a woman. And Deborah arose and went with Barak to Kedesh. [Fulfilled in Judg. 4:22.] And Barak called Zebulun and Naphtali to Kedesh, and he went up with 10,000 men at his heels, and Deborah went up with him. Judges 4:1-10 AMPC*

### 3. Junia was the first woman Apostle.

She was a co-worker in ministry with Paul and Andronicus. The scripture says she was noted among the apostles. The word noted means known, respected, acknowledged, labeled, established, etc. Junia and Andronicus were highly esteemed.

- *Salute Andronicus and Junia, my kinsmen, and my fellowprisoners, who are of note among the apostles, who also were in Christ before me. Romans 16:7 KJV*

### 4. Tryphena, Typhosa, and Persis worked hard for the Lord.

- *Salute those workers in the Lord, Tryphaena and Tryphosa. Greet my dear Persis, who has worked so hard in the Lord. Romans 16:12 AMPC*

Some men will disagree with what's written here, and that's okay! The religious people disagreed with Jesus, but He was correct and righteous in all His ways. If the Scribes and Pharisees found an error in a faultless man and Savior named Jesus, then 21st-century Scribes and Pharisees will find fault with us, His disciples (the people of God). Nonetheless, women taking their rightful position in their homes as godly wives, leaders in the marketplace, and ministry are not salvation issues. But men who are prideful and lack a holy relationship with God are indeed out of bounds with Him. Pride is a salvation issue; ask Satan! Selah! Men are supposed to be godly coverings for women in general and women leaders but not control freaks.

**Scripture references:**

- *In the last days,' God says, 'I will pour out my Spirit upon all people. Your sons and daughters will prophesy. Your young men will see visions, and your old men will dream dreams. Acts of the Apostles 2:17 NLT*

- *And afterward I will pour out My Spirit upon all flesh; and your sons and your daughters shall prophesy, your old men shall dream dreams, your young men shall see visions. Joel 2:28 AMPC*

**Here's a prophetic quote concerning women in ministry:**

*"Jesus Christ allowed Mary to literally pour oil over His entire body. Yet, religious mindsets don't want women to pour oil on the body of Christ spiritually. God was*

*unpacking a mystery for the ages that He always intended for women to pour out on the body of Christ."*

- Apostle Dion Nesmith

# CHAPTER THREE

# Marriage is God's Institution

Marriage is an institution established by God from the beginning of humankind. The marriage institution is a covenant agreement that prophetically represents the body of Christ as the Bride of Christ. God also manufactured (formed, assembled, made) the marriage covenant because He instituted marriage. Since we are at the beginning of this subject matter, I must separate marriages that are honorable to God versus those that aren't. Only marriages that are between born-again males and females are honored by God. The Lord doesn't honor the world's (Satan's) version of marriage. Keep in mind that Satan is the one who continually comes up with alternatives for what God has created and established. Satan can't create, so he perverts what was created by The Almighty God. Nevertheless, unbelievers can live and marry who or what they please, but kingdom men and women must abide by God's kingdom laws, precepts, and righteous restrictions. For the Lord to approve anything we're offering Him or doing in His name, it must be according to His Word, Spirit, and original intent.

A few years ago, the Lord revealed to me that He is our solution to every (not some) problem we have as people. But we keep looking for a solution outside Him to fix our issues. The spiritual covenant of marriage is perfect because God created it. God does all things well! However, when there are issues within a well-crafted marriage covenant, it is because of pride, disobedience, or a lack of surrender from the husband, the wife, or both. We taint what is sacred when we don't follow God's ordinances. To operate within the confines of what Yahweh created, we must return to His Word (the manual for human beings) to find the solution. Only the Word can resolve what He created, not humankind! Yes! God uses people to get His work accomplished on the earth. But those whom He uses, they teach and instruct with His precepts and standards because there's nothing new under the sun (see Ecclesiastes 1:9)! The Word of God works in all situations because it is the Lord's manual for humanity, balance, soundness, maintenance, repair, and for a reset! Selah!

The success of a marriage depends on how well we know the God of the covenant and our surrender to Him. Our marriage to the Lord will determine the level of marriage we will have and maintain with our spouse. No matter how great anyone's marriage is, it is not the standard! The standard for all kingdom marriages is the Word of God. The Word and the leading of the Holy Spirit should always govern every area of our lives and marriages. Many times when a marriage is corrupt, it's because one or two individuals agreed to the covenant without understanding or respecting the standards and weight of the terms and conditions. Intimacy with God causes our spirit to become vexed when we are in error (out of sync with the Lord). We cultivate relationships with godly reverence when we walk in the Holy Spirit. What does this mean? Our daily walk with the Lord governs how we treat our spouse and people. In other words, if we honor the Lord, we will respect people. When we don't reverence God, dishonor (especially to the sacred things of the Lord) is inevitable!

Conviction by the Holy Spirit is essential when we miss the mark (sin). Conviction indicates something is wrong and that we should locate the error, repent, and correct whatever situation God is not pleased with. If most men who profess to be godly would live with this level of humility and sensitivity to God (the Word), then divorce, infidelity, and the like would be minimum or no more. By now, we know the Lord created the marriage covenant. What we further need to know about the covenant is that it is spiritual but lived out in the natural (between male and female). Here's a revelation, covenants created by God must be maintained by His spiritual principles, precepts (the Word of God), and practices. With this in mind, another problem in many marriages is carnal-minded couples bound to a spiritual covenant without understanding the spiritual work required to keep it healthy and holy. Kingdom marriages are supposed to represent the one who created the covenant—God! Individuals submitted to the Lord who get married will produce the fruit of a godly marriage. Couples not surrendered to God in their marriage won't bear good fruit. True believers bear fruit after their kind—Jesus (in singleness and marriage)!

**Here's a passage of scriptures that teach principles that governs that which is spiritual:**

*"But the natural, nonspiritual man does not accept or welcome or admit into his heart the gifts and teachings and revelations of the Spirit of God, for they are folly (meaningless nonsense) to him; and he is incapable of knowing them [of progressively recognizing, understanding, and becoming better acquainted with them] because they are spiritually discerned and estimated and appreciated. But the spiritual man tries all things [he examines, investigates, inquires into, questions, and discerns all things], yet is himself to be put on trial and judged by no one [he can read the meaning of everything, but no one can properly discern or appraise or get an insight into him]. For who has known or understood the mind (the counsels and purposes) of the Lord so as to guide and instruct Him and give Him knowledge? But we have the mind of Christ (the Messiah) and do hold the thoughts (feelings and purposes) of His heart." 1 Corinthians 2:14-16 AMPC*

Those who aren't spiritual don't understand the importance of maintaining a spiritual covenant or spiritual things in general. Because of the lack of knowledge, most professed believers get offended when they hear the truth of God's Word because they have maintained religious practices and man-made traditions but not a covenant relationship with the Lord. When we got saved through receiving Jesus as our Lord and Savior, we agreed to a spiritual covenant, not a religion. A covenant must be maintained for us to get out of it what comes with it. For this reason, we must work out our soul salvation with fear and trembling (see Philippians 2:12). Jesus didn't die for us to receive salvation through Him so we can remain in covenant with Satan through a sinful lifestyle. The covenant of Christ requires us to renew our minds with the Word, walk in the Holy Spirit, live the Word, and do the inward and outward works it takes to birth the results God intended.

**Here's a list of spiritual standards that come with a godly marriage (covenant):**

1. Faithfulness to God
2. Prayer (husbands and wives must maintain a real prayer life individually and collectively)
3. Praise and Worship unto God
4. An individual and joint study of the Word
5. Fasting
6. Self-deliverance and deliverance by a trusted individual as needed
7. Family unity
8. A life (spirit, soul, and body) surrendered entirely to God

Kingdom marriages must be godly spiritual because the enemy hates them. The enemy comes after everything God created, especially unions representing Him. To dismantle the enemy's plots and to survive the attacks against godly marriages, married couples must understand how to defend themselves (as a unit and individually) with the Word and godly spirituality. Men, there's more to marriage than providing financially, attending church, having sex, and making babies. If we don't know God through a personal relationship with Him and His Word, we don't have a spiritual defense for ourselves or our families. If we want true success from God's marriage covenant, we must allow Him to kill our pride, walk in humility and love, cultivate a prayer and fasting lifestyle, study the Word daily, agreement with God and the fullness of His Word.

Men and women are the common denominators in their marriages when they don't understand the covenant they entered. The agreement is more about God and His will than it is about them (the married couple). If we can successfully walk with the Lord, we can successfully walk in agreement with our spouses. As godly leaders of our homes, we should know the God of our salvation and be the kings, prophets, and priests the Lord called us to be for our wives and children. Men, please remember that in the marriage covenant, our wives submit to us as their husbands, but we submit (and remain submitted) to Yahweh! However, if we don't submit to God, we can't expect our wives to submit to us. Here's a deeper reason why: We can only submit to the Lord or Satan but not both simultaneously. We automatically yield to Satan when we don't yield to the Lord. So why would we want our wives submitted to the devil by way of them submitting to us (who refuses to follow God)? Kingdom people don't serve the devil just because they're married to someone who does not or has decided to stop obeying and following the Lord. Whether male or female, our job is to choose God over anything and anyone. Plus, we are all responsible for our soul salvation.

For example, we're supposed to obey the laws of the land. However, if the laws of the land cause us to disobey God, then we're to follow the Lord over the laws (the ungodly laws). Why is this? Because demonic laws are purposely put in place for us to rebel against the Sovereign King. The god of this world (Satan) hates the God of all creation. Satan does everything he can to keep us out of God's will. In the Kingdom of Heaven, God's laws govern all creation. Therefore, if we are citizens of King Yahweh, we abide by His rules and precepts only. There are no other options because kingdom people are committed to the Lord alone. Men of God, are we believers who follow the Word of the Lord or compromisers who follow the god of this world? If we align with the Lord and our wives follow us as the head of our homes, then our wives are led by God through us (the husbands). On the contrary, if we are not walking with God and our spouses are following us, then we are partially responsible for why our spouses have been led away from the ways of the Father to the ways of Satan. For this reason, we must keep God number one in our lives no matter what! We shouldn't ever want to mislead anyone knowingly or unknowingly! Husbands who allow God to lead their lives lead their families in steps that the Lord orders. Let those with spiritual ears hear what the Spirit of the Lord is saying to His people! Selah!

# CHAPTER FOUR

# Men After God's Own Heart

If we are men of the Word, we know of one king and priest who was also a prophet God called "A man after His own heart." His name is David! Three essential things (but not limited to the three I mention) about David caused Him to be a man after God's heart. David repented of his sins, walked humbly, and remained a true worshipper of Yahweh. David wasn't double-minded about who he worshipped. God loves humanity, and His will is for all to repent (change our hearts and minds about our sins) and turn to Him. Actual change (repentance) keeps us in right standing with the Lord. Repentance brings restoration to our souls and keeps our spiritual doors closed so that demon spirits don't have access (legal, spiritual access) to us through unrepentant sin.

*"The Lord does not delay and is not tardy or slow about what He promises, according to some people's conception of slowness, but He is long-suffering (extraordinarily patient) toward you, not desiring that any should perish, but that all should turn to repentance." 2 Peter 3:9 AMPC*

Many men (saved and unsaved) have a big issue with living humble lives before the Lord. We need to know that God resists the proud but exalts the humble (see James 4:6). If we don't want to be demoted by the Lord, we must stay humble. A part of humility is admitting we are wrong, apologizing for our errors (mistakes), and not thinking too highly of ourselves. In other words, we should never have an exaggerated opinion of our importance (see Romans 12:3 AMPC). It doesn't make us weak when we acknowledge our mistakes. However, it does make us accountable. David wasn't a weak man by far! He owned his errors (which were many) and consistently made sure He was in right standing with the Lord (through repentance and turning from his sin). Yahweh continued to bless David's children even after his death due to his faithfulness toward Him. We honor the Lord when we obey Him but dishonor Him when we don't. A man who refuses to admit when he's wrong is full of pride but also resisted by the Lord. We must stay humble if we want to remain on the good side of God's judgment.

**Scripture references:**

- *Humble yourselves therefore under the mighty hand of God, that he may exalt you in due time: casting all your care upon Him; for He careth for you. 1 Peter 5:6-7 KJV*

- *Pride goes before destruction, and haughtiness before a fall. Proverbs 16:18 NLT*

- *But he giveth more grace. Wherefore he saith, God resisteth the proud, but giveth grace unto the humble. James 4:6 KJV*

- *Jesus said unto him, it is written again, thou shalt not tempt the Lord thy God. Matthew 4:7 KJV*

An unconditional worshipper of Yahweh (one who worships Him through the good and bad times) is essential for being a man after His heart. Many professed believers (especially men) don't have a problem with worshipping God until they find out He requires us to completely give up our old lifestyle to put on a new life in Christ. True worship that God requires can't include pride or any unrepentant sin. But worship must encompass quality time (intimacy) in His presence, His Word, and a surrendered life unto Him. We can't worship God correctly without understanding His non-negotiable standards and requirements. In addition, we can't be worshippers (one who possesses a lifestyle of worship) of God without intimacy, and we can't please Him and live in pride simultaneously. Therefore, pride and a lack of closeness with the Lord are two areas that keep men from excelling in their walk with Him.

Ungodly examples of manhood prevent many men from having a great relationship with the Father. If most men examine themselves, they will find out they don't have a problem displaying emotions and outward expressions of worship because men show great passion and reverence for the things they love and value. Selah! When our emotions and expressions of worship are misplaced, we offer them to someone or something else (sports, women, cars, houses, etc.) but not their rightful owner (Yahweh). Worship is not attending church every Sunday and even serving in a ministry. We can do all the religious works and live worse than unbelievers (many professed believers do). We're true worshippers when we worship in spirit and truth (void of all falsities). We're also true worshippers when the totality of our lives (spirit, soul, and body) agrees with God. Worshipping God is not an act but a daily lifestyle that includes godly morals, His Word, and productivity, representing each person's assignment from the Lord.

*"I beseech you therefore, brethren, by the mercies of God, that ye present your bodies a living sacrifice, holy, acceptable unto God, which is your reasonable service. And be not conformed to this world: but be ye transformed by the renewing of your mind, that ye may prove what is that good, and acceptable, and perfect, will of God."*
*Romans 12:1-2 KJV*

As kingdom men, we must address that, more times than none, we respond to carnal things better than God. Our actions indicate we have a relational issue with the Lord. If we can be super enthusiastic about sports, women, and other things, then we owe the Lord exceedingly more enthusiasm because of who He is (the Sovereign King and Creator)! The absence of intimacy and excitement for God equals a relationship on life support waiting to flatline. David was one of the greatest and fiercest warriors of the Lord during his time on the earth. He was also a musician, psalmist, songwriter, and a man who danced before the Lord unashamedly with all his might. None of David's expressions toward God made him less of a man. David loved God, and he wasn't afraid to show it. When he messed up, he repented to the Father and kept moving forward as a man after God's heart. King David was also highly favored by the Lord.

*"So David decided not to move the Ark of the Lord into the City of David. Instead, he took it to the house of Obed-edom of Gath. The Ark of the Lord remained there in Obed-edom's house for three months, and the Lord blessed Obed-edom and his entire household. Then King David was told, "The Lord has blessed Obed-edom's household and everything he has because of the Ark of God." So David went there and brought the Ark of God from the house of Obed-edom to the City of David with a great celebration. After the men who were carrying the Ark of the Lord had gone six steps, David sacrificed a bull and a fattened calf. And David danced before the Lord with all his might, wearing a priestly garment. So David and all the people of Israel brought up the Ark of the Lord with shouts of joy and the blowing of rams' horns." 2 Samuel 6:10-15 NLT*

How passionate are we about the Lord and His presence? To know the Lord and to feel His presence is a privilege and an honor. We serve the most amazing God EVER! Every other god is a counterfeit! There's no one like the Lord, and He deserves our praise and worship daily! As men, we aren't exempt from surrendering our hearts to the Lord. Where there's intimacy with God, depth is inevitable! Where there's depth, there is spiritual soundness. Where there's soundness, there's the Word. Where the Word is, there's Jesus because He is the living Word! A relationship with Yahweh changes and sustains every area of our lives. All men can be men after God's heart if we genuinely repent from our sins, stay humble, and passionately worship (with our spirit, soul, and body) the King of Glory!

# CHAPTER FIVE

# Men With Diverse Gifts & Skills

We need to know that everything God gave us is His intent (on purpose for a purpose). He didn't make a mistake! Our job is always to take the plan of God and move our lives forward with it by the leading of the Holy Spirit and the Word. God doesn't waste anything, and our responsibility is not to waste what He gave us. That said, all of humanity has gifts and skill sets that differ. Our gifts are not exclusive to us because the Lord has given others the same gifts. But how we flow and operate our gifts is exclusively for us because God created us as originals and not counterfeits (false versions of others).

God has given each person something they can do easily without formal training. Most of us can do two to three things well without formal education. These natural abilities indicate that we have gifts in need of cultivating. Our job is to mature our gifts and continue to elevate them. From our God-given gifts, we can build and produce other skills or products that generate multiple income streams. No matter our gifts, we're not more manly because of them. We individually have gifts wrapped in purpose by God so we can do His will in the earth. We benefit from our gifts, but our natural abilities bless others more than they bless us. In like manner, other people's gifts help us more than they help them. Therefore, we need each other! Every gift has a purpose that produces a good return if we put time into developing that gift. In addition, every gift has expansion hidden in it, enabling growth and new opportunities

Therefore, we should never despise or overlook small things or the beginning stages of small beginnings because the seed of the Lord (planted in us) is waiting for us to bring it to maturity. The maturation of gifts and abilities opens us up for multiplication (more). There is no joy or fulfillment like doing what God has gifted us. But if we get caught up in trying to be like the next man, we will miss out on the greatness the Lord intended for us to birth in the earth. We should pursue our God-given gifts and talents because many people need what we have. No one can do what we do the way we do it! God created a variety of abilities on purpose!

In Exodus 25:10-40, God spoke to Moses and had him instruct the children of Israel on how the Ark of the Covenant should be built. It took men who He anointed, appointed, and gifted to build such an excellent work of art to hold the tablets of the covenant. In that passage of scripture, we see the art and skills of carpentry and goldsmith (one who specializes in working with gold and other precious metals) at its best. In Exodus 31:1-11, the Lord anointed Bezalel with great wisdom, ability, and expertise in all kinds of crafts. Bezalel was a master craftsman in engraving, mounting precious gemstones, and carving wood. Bezalel and his assistant Oholiab also made and decorated the curtains for the tabernacle. In addition, the craftsmen (Bezalel and Oholiab) also made elaborate priestly robes for Aaron and his sons to wear.

As mentioned earlier, David was a skilled musician, songwriter, singer, and warrior. Throughout the Word of God, we see many individuals (especially men) who God gifted with various skills and abilities. Our assignment is to take what God has given us and use it to our fullest capacity. What is all this conveying? It confirms that God didn't make any mistakes by giving us the natural abilities we have. Whether God calls you to build an ark like Noah, play like David, or make clothes like Bezalel, be free to use every gift and skill the Lord gave you. It doesn't make us more or less of a man because of our diverse skill(s) and abilities given by the Lord. However, it does make us accountable, innovative, and responsible when we use what the Most High God gave us instead of wasting it due to wanting what the next man has. Remember, there is an unexplainable feeling of joy, peace, and satisfaction (with expansion) when we do what God has naturally gifted us. We individually have what we have on purpose for a purpose. That purpose includes our prosperity and the upbuilding of God's kingdom with our spheres of influence through our gifts and talents.

# Don't Sacrifice Your Call on the Alter of False Peace & Acceptance

At this time, we all know that we have gifts and skills that the Lord has given us. But each of us also has a specific call of God. Before God created a wife for Adam, he was in right standing with Him. Adam knew what the Lord called him to do (see Genesis 1: 26-30). As kingdom men, we need to develop our walk with the Lord, the work the Lord chooses us to do, and the purpose for why we are here. These areas are essential for us to know before we get married so that we can make sober decisions in life. We can't make sober decisions apart from understanding who we are and our purpose (God's purpose). When we don't understand these areas, we will marry someone who doesn't have the grace to complement the call of God on our lives. According to Genesis 2:18, God created Adam, a helper meet (wife) that was suitable, adapted, and complementary for him. The Lord created Adam, a wife according to who He made him to be and to accomplish.

The will of the Lord is to make sure we are clear about who we are before entering a marriage covenant. Why is this important? So that we don't marry anyone outside the covenant of Jesus Christ, whom I call foreigners (unbelievers of all sorts). When we know who we are, we make godly decisions according to our purpose and not ungodly decisions led by our lust. Selah! Some men and women got married without knowing the call of God for their life. They later came into the knowledge of their calling (after becoming serious about their walk with the Lord), but their spouses weren't interested in their newfound call of God (which they always had). Nevertheless, the individuals who revealed the call of God to their spouses had to make a hard decision to obey God or please their spouses. Unfortunately, they chose their spouse's desires over God's to keep the peace in their homes and marriages. Most individuals follow their spouses to avoid drama, but the will of God overrides everything and everyone. A spouse (a "creation" of God) is not more important than Yahweh! We must pursue who the Lord called us to be at all costs.

Civil warfare within marriage is one of the main reasons we must have a real relationship with the Lord, know what He had called us to do, and pursue His will before we say "I do" to anyone! It's one thing to sacrifice things to keep peace in a marriage, but it's a whole different situation when we sacrifice the call of God. Selah! We should never compromise our walk with the Lord and His call on our lives for anyone unless we're willing to rebel against the Father. On the contrary, if we stop pursuing the Lord because our spouse doesn't want to level up in Him (mature in the Word and godliness), our spouse has become our idol god, which is idolatry! When we rush into making major life decisions before understanding who we are in Christ, we create significant problems for ourselves. But there are no problems too complicated for the Lord. As followers of the Way (Jesus), we will passionately serve God whether our spouses approve of our walk with the Lord. Our marriage to God should never end in divorce! Selah!

We can't afford to allow anyone to distract us from living out the Lord's purpose for our lives. Many men and women are in this situation, but we must choose God and trust Him with the outcome. After all, we are alive for His purpose and not our own! He can change our situation for the better without switching out our spouses. However, sometimes situations call for us to end a marriage God never approved us to enter. Whatever the case, we must follow the Word and the Spirit of the Lord. When God is not the first option in our lives, we make costly mistakes like marrying someone who doesn't have the grace that compliments who the Lord called us to be. Men of God, don't sacrifice your call on the altar of false peace and acceptance. But pursue the Lord and His will with all diligence. Real peace comes with obeying God and carrying out His will and purpose in the earth. We will all give an account for doing the will of the Lord or for not doing His will.

Nevertheless, we cannot use this excuse: "My wife wasn't interested in me seriously perusing you, Lord, so I stopped just to keep peace in my home." Remember, hearing "servant well done" from the Lord is completely different than hearing it from a spouse or friend who manipulated you out of His will. Once more, if your wife carries more weight in your life than the Almighty God, you have an idol before Him (and vice versa)!

CHAPTER SIX

# Negligent Influence

The word negligent means to slack at taking proper care of a thing or person. The synonyms for negligent are careless, thoughtless, sloppy, and irresponsible. One of the things the Lord wants me to bring awareness to in the body of Christ is the importance of His people representing Him well to other believers and unbelievers. Many men (and women) are leaders in high-level positions of influence in ministry, but their level of godly maturity is surface (depthless, insignificant, small). The higher we ascend in different mountains of influence in the world or God's kingdom, the more we must die to ourselves (live very humbly) daily and become more like Christ. For example, the higher we ascend, the thinner the air becomes. In other words, the amount of oxygen in the air decreases as we go upwards, hindering our ability to breathe normally. The higher the Lord takes us, the humbler we should become instead of becoming pompous (arrogant) and prideful. As kingdom men, we shouldn't walk through doors of influence and decide it's okay to lose our reverence for the Lord once we become popular. There are many men in key leadership positions in the body of Christ who represents the Lord with such negligence from a big platform. The Lord wants us to remember this: *"To whom much is given, much is required (see Luke 12:48)."* The more influential we become, the more responsible we must be as believers because we represent the Almighty God! The judgment of the Lord will be greater on ministry leaders than the laity because much is given to them by God, and much is required of them by Him!

Many men in pastoral and other positions do a horrible job representing the Lord and the body of Christ. These same leaders have been leading their large congregations away from the fear, reverence, and standards of the Lord to fleshly carnality and sinful practices. Since many people are looking for ways to retrieve the blessings of the Lord without having to obey Him, a great majority of the laity goes along with the negligence of these leaders because they are either of the exact nature or ignorant of the expectations of the Lord. As men, we are natural leaders in our homes, the marketplace, or ministry. However, if we are kingdom men of God, how we walk, talk, and act should represent Christ, not Satan. Here's an essential impartation, the greater the Lord elevates us in different areas and spheres of influence, the more restricted our walk with Him must become. We can no longer do certain things we used to do because more people are watching us and looking to us as role models.

No matter how small or significant our influence is, we can lead people righteously (by the unadulterated Word of God) or on a path of carnality that leads to death. Whether we know it or not, we will give an account for every person we influence down the right or wrong path (knowingly and unknowingly). If people go in the wrong direction due to our negligence, their blood will be on our hands. Always remember that authentic kingdom citizens are ambassadors for Christ. Jesus' ambassadors are full-time representatives of Yahweh. We didn't (and shouldn't) get saved to gain the title of Christian merely. Instead, we came into salvation through Jesus and inherited a royal lifestyle because our God is the King of Glory! The lifestyle of a believer is a lifestyle of royalty. Therefore, our identity in Christ is God's royal priesthood. The lifestyle of kings and priests is a consecrated life unto the Lord. Anything or a consecrated person is set apart for a special use. That said, believers are instructed by the Word to live set-apart lives unto the Lord and to demonstrate His lifestyle, Word, power, and purpose to humanity.

*"But ye are a chosen generation, a royal priesthood, an holy nation, a peculiar people; that ye should shew forth*

*the praises of him who hath called you out of darkness into his marvelous light:" 1 Peter 2:9 KJV*

I conclude we shouldn't use our free will to misrepresent the Lord. No number of followers, fame, money, and the like are worth having to give an account for the people we misled with our ungodly negligence. We must know that just because something is permissible for us doesn't mean it is helpful for us to do. Always consider the price that comes with careless influence and the misrepresentation of the Lord to people who don't know the difference between right and wrong.

*"Everything is permissible (allowable and lawful) for me; but not all things are helpful (good for me to do, expedient and profitable when considered with other things). Everything is lawful for me, but I will not become the slave of anything or be brought under its power." 1 Corinthians 6:12 AMPC*

# Godly Male Confidants

It's no secret that most men hide their inner life (motives, thoughts, desires), emotions, and personal experiences. I didn't make a typo when I wrote "emotions." Yes! I know it's shocking, but men have emotions! God created humanity (male and female) with the ability to feel. Emotions are a part of the human soul, made up of our mind, will, and emotions. Our emotions allow us to feel, express passion, and exude excitement. Our emotions also give us the ability to release and feel the affection of others as well as express desires, sympathy, instinct, etc. There's a difference between expressing emotions versus being emotional. It's natural for men to express emotions, but it's abnormal to be emotionless. Regarding women's emotions, they are more emotionally driven than men due to how God made them. Women are nurturers by nature which makes them more emotional than men. On the contrary, men are more collected, laid-back, and stern, which causes them to release emotions differently than women. However, as human beings, our emotions will be taken out of balance when the Word does not maintain our spirit, soul (mind, will, emotions), and body. When it comes to the inner life (motives, thoughts, desires) and personal experiences of men, many don't have the right men in their lives who allow them to honestly release what they've been holding in for days, months, and even years. Countless men take hard falls in life because they lack godly accountability to instruct them in wise—godly counsel. Men and women alike were created by God for community and not permanent long rangers.

As men of God, we need healthy—godly male confidants in our lives because there are conversations and situations only we can understand. That same fact goes for women. I admit we must operate in the wisdom of the Lord when choosing confidants because godly integrity is the key component. It's great to have at least one to two male figures in our lives with whom we can confess our faults (interchangeably) so we can receive the healing and restoration as James 5:16 instructs us. Godly confidants listen well and offer wise counsel from the Word of the Lord. Receiving the wrong counsel can be detrimental to us in many ways.

**Here's four scriptures that reveals the importance of a confidant and wise counselors:**

- *Confess to one another therefore your faults (your slips, your false steps, your offenses, your sins) and pray [also] for one another, that you may be healed and restored [to a spiritual tone of mind and heart]. The earnest (heartfelt, continued) prayer of a righteous man makes tremendous power available [dynamic in its working]. James 5:16 AMPC*

- *Blessed (happy, fortunate, prosperous, and enviable) is the man who walks and lives not in the counsel of the ungodly [following their advice, their plans and purposes], nor stands [submissive and inactive] in the path where sinners walk, nor sits down [to relax and rest] where the scornful [and the mockers] gather. Psalm 1:1 AMPC*

- *The way of a fool is right in his own eyes, but he who listens to counsel is wise. Proverbs 12:15 AMPC*

- *Where there is no [wise, intelligent] guidance, the people fall [and go off course like a ship without a helm], But in the abundance of [wise and godly] counselors there is victory. Proverbs 11:14 AMP*

Believers live in the light and not darkness. This truth doesn't mean we won't need the counsel of the Lord or a moment to vent to a male confidant because we will! Life happens! Plus, the Word tells us to bare one another's burdens (see Galatians 6:2). While life happens, we must have safeguards in place (starting with God first and people of value) so that our enemy won't use our dysfunctions (a manufactured inability to communicate well with undeveloped emotional health) against us during an intense moment of temptation. One of the most important things to know about our enemies (Satan and his demonic spirits) is that they love for us to hide our secrets when we make sinful mistakes or indulge in sin. If Satan can keep us away from our support system during a vulnerable moment, he and his demon spirits can take us out (influence us to end our life) with guilt and shame. It happens more often than it ever should! We must maintain a vigorous walk with the Lord, which includes eating (studying) the Word daily because it keeps the enemy from taking advantage of us due to a lack of knowledge. The Word of God is a Divine Keeper!

Moreover, maintaining a healthy relationship with one or two kingdom men is important because all men aren't married, which means they don't have spousal support like some men. But even if men are married, they still need other men for godly community purposes. When we have confidants in place, we realize we're not the only ones dealing with complex issues because they either have the same problems, had them in the past, or know someone currently wrestling with the same issues. That alone brings great relief because Satan makes us think we are the only ones suffering in certain areas. Men of God, decide today that this is the last day you will go through life without having the right circle of godly mentors. You owe it to yourself! Don't allow the enemy to keep you trapped in things that cause mental health issues due to a lack of repentance, forgiveness, and access to others with whom you can share your struggles. Remember, godly men walk in the light of Christ and not darkness (sin). It's time for men to receive restoration of spiritual and emotional health (through a personal encounter with God) so that they can connect intimately with the Lord, themselves, their wives and children, and others.

*"BRETHREN, IF any person is overtaken in misconduct or sin of any sort, you who are spiritual [who are responsive to and controlled by the Spirit] should set him right and restore and reinstate him, without any sense of superiority and with all gentleness, keeping an attentive eye on yourself, lest you should be tempted also. Bear (endure, carry) one another's burdens and troublesome moral faults, and in this way fulfill and observe perfectly the law of Christ (the Messiah) and complete what is lacking [in your obedience to it]. For if any person thinks himself to be somebody [too important to condescend to shoulder another's load] when he is nobody [of superiority except in his own estimation], he deceives and deludes and cheats himself." Galatians 6:1-3 AMPC*

# CHAPTER SEVEN

# The Dangers of Idolatry

When our relationship with God is personal, and we know His Word, we know that idolatry and Yahweh (God) don't mix. In God's kingdom, He is the "only" one we worship because He warns us to have no other god before Him (see Exodus 20:3 and Exodus 34:14). God created all creation to worship Him. But because of the free will granted to us by the Lord, we get to choose to worship Him or Satan. However, if we are going to be a part of God's kingdom, the totality of our lives must align with His Word and ways without any exceptions or opinions. In addition, by God's design, everything in His kingdom reflects and reveals His glory. We're never to worship what the Lord created or be bound to ungodly oaths (covenants, agreement, pledges, etc.) that connects us to evil spirits, false gods, etc. Everything that Yahweh calls immoral, wrong, demonic, and the like is ungodly! Sins of any sort will not enter the Kingdom of God. However, due to the lack of teaching and abiding in the Word, many believers have invited familiar spirits (demons) into their lives because they don't know the Lord or His standards. Religion results in the teaching of man-made doctrines (and parts of the Bible that don't challenge believers to level up), denominations, and traditions that nullify the power of God instead of how to maintain an intimate relationship with the Father through Jesus. In addition, new age, idolatry, witchcraft, divination, and the like has become the norm among many believers who profess Christ. Even most of the ministry teachings and sermons we hear today are about what God can do for us instead of what we're supposed to do for Him.

Many men of God consider themselves believers but are involved in unholy things and ungodly covenants the Lord hates! We are lukewarm when we live a not hot or cold life. If we're neither of the two, then we are lukewarm. We are lukewarm when we claim Jesus but live like or worse than unbelievers. For example, coffee is offered hot or cold but never lukewarm. No one in their right mind wants lukewarm coffee! Yuck! Whenever someone gives me warm coffee, I spit it out immediately upon drinking it.

In comparison, God does the same! The Word says in Revelation 3:15-17 AMPC, *"I know your [record of] works and what you are doing; you are neither cold nor hot. Would that you were cold or hot! So, because you are lukewarm and neither cold nor hot, I will spew you out of My mouth! For you say, I am rich; I have prospered and grown wealthy, and I am in need of nothing; and you do not realize and understand that you are wretched, pitiable, poor, blind, and naked."*

If we are faithful kingdom men, idolatry and other occult practices should never be a part of our lives. We ensure God is first, and we're not attached to anything that offends Him. On the contrary, if we're lukewarm or ignorant of Satan's devices, we are easily offended when someone confronts us about our idols, witchcraft, sexual immorality, and sin in general. For the sake of clarity, idols are not just stone statues. Idols are anything or anyone we highly praise and place more attention, time, and effort on than the Lord. In the world's kingdoms (and a segment of the body of Christ), the lust of the flesh, the lust of the eyes, and the pride of life are all popular idols of our time.

*"For all that is in the world–the lust of the flesh [craving for sensual gratification] and the lust of the eyes [greedy longings of the mind] and the pride of life [assurance in one's own resources or in the stability of earthly things]– these do not come from the Father but are from the world [itself]." 1 John 2:16 AMPC*

**Here's a list of widespread idolatry and religious practices (but not limited to this list) that made their way into the body of Christ:**

1. The worship of ministry leaders, singers, musicians, and secular artists alike (they are made more important than God)
2. Theology doctorate degrees and degrees in general (there's nothing wrong with degrees, but we should not place our confidence in them because it belongs to God)
3. Spiritual fathers and mothers (many give more reverence and honor to spiritual parents than God)
4. Honor (we should never expect or want people to honor us when they don't honor the Lord. Honoring humanity (no matter who they are) is inevitable when we live in honor of the Most High God).
5. The celebration of pagan holidays (most holidays are rooted in paganism which God hates)
6. Fraternities and sororities, masons and eastern stars, and any other secret society (all "secret" societies are idolatrous organizations with spiritual rituals and oaths that binds individuals to false gods that are ancient demonic spirits)
7. Mental health therapist (godly Mental Health Therapist are great and very much needed. But many people have more confidence, reverence, and faith in them than God and His Word)
8. Influential leaders and celebrities (a large majority of believers defend people who are popular with such conviction, but they never defend the Lord with the same zeal and passion)
9. Sports and entertainment (there's an extraordinary anticipation and preparation for sports and entertainment that many don't have for God. In addition, most believers will give their last dime to attend sports and concert events, but they will not

provide or give much to support the local church, needy people, and the kingdom of God)

10. The worship of "self" and "money" (the Words say, "You should know this, Timothy, that in the last days, there will be very difficult times. For people will love only themselves and their money. They will be boastful and proud, scoffing at God, disobedient to their parents, and ungrateful. They will consider nothing sacred.") 2 Timothy 3:1-2 NLT

11. African Spirituality (a religion that worships dead ancestors, which are demonic spirits that are familiar to us and our families)

12. All types of occult crystals (many people look to rocks from the earth to heal, protect, bless, and the like instead of Jesus)

13. Ethnicity Idolatry (when our skin color becomes superior)

This accurate list may seem a bit much to some men and people, but it's very informative to many who don't know and are ready to correct their wrongs. However, for disciples of Christ, it's the truth that confirms how desperately we need God because many of us have fallen away from His will and Word. We must destroy all demonic covenants, oaths, pledges, false gods, and idolatry. It doesn't matter if we are very successful in the world; if we are doing or a part of anything mentioned in the list above, we are out of alignment with God. It also means we have demonic doors open in our lives, and we have to shut them immediately through prayer by confessing our sins and renouncing our evil practices.

Moreover, worldly success doesn't mean we are right with the Father. Truthfully, we can gain the whole world and lose our souls to Satan (see Matthew 16:26). It's not about what we or anyone else thinks about what this chapter covers. It is all about what God and His Word say. There is zero tolerance for the thirteen things mentioned above in the Kingdom of

God. The Lord will not share His glory with anything or anyone! If we are guilty, we can repent (to turn completely away from what God hates by changing our minds) and turn entirely to the Word and standards of God. Repent and be restored in Jesus' name! The grace of Jesus is always sufficient, and He's ready to restore us instantly.

# Idolatry Versus Personal Conviction

Anytime we use "That's not my personal conviction" as a defense to cover and maintain what God calls idolatry (or sin in general), we're saying idolatry is idolatry based on how "we" feel about it or whether "we" are convicted by our actions. If this is our thought process, it is far from the truth! God calls idolatry sin whether we know it is a sin or not or if our sin convicts us. We don't get to alter (change) what the Lord calls right or wrong. Personal convictions are about our relationship with God and what He and His Word tell us to do or not do because of our level of influence or spiritual maturity. For example, the Holy Spirit will convict us about not doing a particular thing (not because it is a sin) because it will cause someone who respects us (due to our influence) to stumble and fall into sin by copying what they saw us do or thought we did. The wrong perception of a thing creates much confusion and deception. The Word says, *"With all thy getting, get an understanding (see Proverbs 4:7)."*

Moreover, mature believers live their lives with discretion. The Lord tells us in His Word to abstain from the very presence of evil (see 1 Thessalonians 5:22). We cannot do what we see the next person do and vice versa, no matter how popular or free they are to do a thing. We must not be negligent with our influence and freedom because we are responsible for who we lead astray from the ways of God. We should never want to influence anyone to go down the wrong path, knowingly or unknowingly.

As I stated previously, idolatry is idolatry! But personal convictions are personal to us as individuals and according to our relationship with God. In addition, our personal convictions aren't written in the Bible as God's laws and precepts. But humanity is warned against the dangers of idolatry throughout the Old and New Testaments. What God considers idolatry doesn't change from person to person. Everything the Word calls sin and idolatry is sin and idolatry! It doesn't matter if we or our favorite people are practicing what God hates; if He says it is wrong, that settles it! Our status or popularity doesn't change the truth and standards the Lord set. We are mere mortals, not the Sovereign God!

Lastly, when it comes to serving, we cannot use community service and leadership as "idolatry validation." Some of the most popular world and ministry leaders are big charitable givers but also idolaters and sorcerers (those who practice witchcraft). We can't be authentic kingdom men and women of God and be in oaths to another god(s). That's completely forbidden! However, religious people, witchcraft practitioners, and those who are not real kingdom ambassadors for Christ do as they please because they serve another god. We can work for the Lord without ever surrendering our lives to Him. Selah! True worship is saying "yes" to God about everything He requires of us and "no" to everything He hates! The Kingdom of God has no "a la carte" options! What do I mean? A la carte is the practice of ordering individual products we want from a menu while leaving the rest (what we don't want). There is no middle option with the Lord! We can either do things His way or Satan's.

**Scripture references:**

- *But as for the cowards and unbelieving and abominable [who are devoid of character and personal integrity and practice or tolerate immorality], and murderers, and sorcerers [with intoxicating drugs], and idolaters and occultists [who practice and teach false religions], and all the liars [who knowingly deceive and twist truth], their part will be in the lake that blazes with fire and brimstone, which is the second death. Revelation 21:8 AMP*

- *Now the practices of the sinful nature are clearly evident: they are sexual immorality, impurity, sensuality (total irresponsibility, lack of self-control), idolatry, sorcery, hostility, strife, jealousy, fits of anger, disputes, dissensions, factions [that promote heresies], envy, drunkenness, riotous behavior, and other things like these. I warn you beforehand, just as I did previously, that those who practice such things will not inherit the kingdom of God. Galatians 5:19-21 AMP*

- *Not everyone who says to Me, Lord, Lord, will enter the kingdom of heaven, but he who does the will of My Father Who is in heaven. Many will say to Me on that day, Lord, Lord, have we not prophesied in Your name and driven out demons in Your name and done many mighty works in Your name? And then I will say to them openly (publicly), I never knew you; depart from Me, you who act wickedly [disregarding My commands]. Matthew 7:21-23 AMPC*

- *If you [really] love Me, you will keep (obey) My commands. John 14:15 AMPC*

# CHAPTER EIGHT

# Sexual Immorality Part 1

Sex is always a big topic of discussion whether a man is a believer or an unbeliever. However, when we become saved and married, worldly things and practices we learned about sex must be addressed and resolved. The lifestyle practices of an unbeliever versus a believer are countercultural (completely different). But without a consistent mind renewal of the Word, we will continue in old behaviors that aren't becoming a man of God. In the world, everything goes! Especially ungodly sexual behaviors and habits because lawlessness is the standard for unbelievers. But in the Kingdom of God, there are righteous restrictions within the standard of holiness. In the body of Christ, sexual immorality is at an all-time high because many men (and women) have not fully surrendered their spirit, soul, and body to the Lord. Sexual sin is not practiced merely among single men but by married men too! As believers, single men shouldn't engage in any sexual activity at any time. Many single brothers profess Christ but justify their sexual relationships because of urges they continue to feed. In their minds, it's okay! However, sexual immorality goes entirely against God's Word and is also an issue of salvation. The good news is this, no matter the sin we're in, we still have time to get it right with the Lord. That time is now! God didn't promise us tomorrow!

**Here's what the Word of God says:**

- *Let there be no sexual immorality, impurity, or greed among you. Such sins have no place among God's people. Ephesians 5:3 NLT*

- *When you follow the desires of your sinful nature, the results are very clear: sexual immorality, impurity, lustful pleasures, idolatry, sorcery, hostility, quarreling, jealousy, outbursts of anger, selfish ambition, dissension, division, envy, drunkenness, wild parties, and other sins like these. Let me tell you again, as I have before, that anyone living that sort of life will not inherit the Kingdom of God. But the Holy Spirit produces this kind of fruit in our lives: love, joy, peace, patience, kindness, goodness, faithfulness, gentleness, and self-control. There is no law against these things! Galatians 5:19-23 NLT*

- *I can hardly believe the report about the sexual immorality going on among you—something that even pagans don't do. I am told that a man in your church is living in sin with his stepmother. 1 Corinthians 5:1 NLT*

- *God's will is for you to be holy, so stay away from all sexual sin. 1 Thessalonians 4:3 NLT*

- *When I wrote to you before, I told you not to associate with people who indulge in sexual sin. But I wasn't talking about unbelievers who indulge in sexual sin, or are greedy, or cheat people, or worship idols. You would have to leave this world to avoid people like that. I meant that you are not to associate with anyone who claims to be a believer yet indulges in sexual sin, or is greedy, or worships idols, or is abusive, or is a drunkard, or cheats people. Don't even eat with such people. 1 Corinthians 5:9-11 NLT*

- *Do you not know that the unrighteous and the wrongdoers will not inherit or have any share in the kingdom of God? Do not be deceived (misled): neither the impure and immoral, nor idolaters, nor adulterers, nor those who participate in homosexuality, Nor cheats (swindlers and thieves), nor greedy graspers, nor drunkards, nor foulmouthed revilers and slanderers, nor extortioners and robbers will inherit or have any share in the kingdom of God. And such some of you were [once]. But you were washed clean (purified by a complete atonement for sin and made free from the guilt of sin), and you were consecrated (set apart, hallowed), and you were justified [pronounced righteous, by trusting] in the name of the Lord Jesus Christ and in the [Holy] Spirit of our God. 1 Corinthians 6:9-11 AMPC*

As you can see, the Word has much to say about sexual immorality. The scriptures above are just a few, but there are many more scriptures about sexual immorality in the Word. After receiving Christ, many saved men kept the worldly mindset that "they must fulfill their sexual needs." *But if any man be in Christ, he is a new creature: old things are passed away; behold all things are new (see 2 Corinthians 5:17).* If we are genuinely saved, we have the power to obey everything that's written in God's Word which includes staying away from fornication. Unsanctioned sexual activity goes against the will of the Lord, and it has significant spiritual and detrimental consequences. Yes! Sexual activity feels good to our flesh, but is it worth losing our soul salvation (if we don't repent from our sins)? Absolutely not! Once saved is not always saved! Faithful kingdom men live within the confines of God's Word and not the standards of Satan (the standards of the world). When they mess up, they repent quickly and return to God's righteousness and holiness.

Satan loves for us to engage in sexual immorality because he knows it worships him. Satan also knows that sexual immorality keeps us bound and separated from God by keeping us out of His will (see Isaiah 59:1-2). We can't serve God and live in open or hidden sin simultaneously. Galatians 5:9 warns us that sexual immorality is sinful, but the Holy Spirit produces self-control. The way out of sexual sin is to repent (a change of mind), obey the Word, fully surrender to the Lord (spirit, soul, and body), and constantly walk in the Holy Spirit. We are not hungry for what we don't continuously feed ourselves. Selah! Does that statement mean we will never have sexual urges if we stop having sex outside of marriage? No, because we will! However, those urges won't be as intense and frequent. Do single men have to fulfill their sexual urges? No! If they had to, the Lord would have never told us all to stay away from fornication (adultery, sexual immorality, etc.) or given us the option to remain single instead of making marriage mandatory. We have the power of God (through the Holy Spirit) to control ourselves. We're supposed to control our bodies instead of our bodies controlling us. The Word says we are the slave of whatever controls us (see 2 Peter 2:19).

Several ministry leaders preach that sexual immorality is okay. They affirm unauthorized sexual and other ungodly practices because they are sexually immoral and adulterous. For many ministry leaders to feel normal about their sexual immorality and adulterous lifestyle, they legalize sex outside of marriage to the laity (sheep, church members) when God has deemed it illegal. As a man, I understand how sexual urges and temptations feel. But I also understand the purpose of evil and how being out of the Father's will harms our lives now and later. This message is not about being religious. But it is about being integral to God and intentional about keeping ourselves out of sexual sin. Illegal sexual practices harm our soul (mind, will, and emotions) and body because they give demon spirits legal rights to oppress and keep us in a place of spiritual and mental torment. Lastly, the kingdom covenant of the Lord is of royalty, holiness, justice, and righteousness. The covenant of Satan is of sin, sexual immorality, witchcraft, rebellion, perversion, and idolatry. Each person chooses to live the life that aligns with the agreement (the covenant of Christ or Satan) they decided to enter. Remember, the covenant of Christ is life, and the covenant of Satan is death.

# Sexual Immorality Part 2

Regarding sexual immorality, it's essential to know that it goes beyond having sex outside of marriage. Synonyms for immorality are corrupt, sinful, impure, perverted, wrong, improper, ungodly, unclean, and the like. With this list in mind, pornography, and masturbation falls under the category of sexual immorality. Every man is or has been guilty of these two areas at some point in their life. I was guilty for years until God revealed that neither pleases Him because they are sinful practices. Not only are pornography and masturbation sexually immoral, but they are also acts of perversion. Anything we do that goes against God's original intent is either perversion or a form of perversion. Immoral practices are sins whether we are single or married. We can't watch pornography without the spirit of lust and perversion being present. For married men, adultery happens in the mind before it occurs naturally. Sin generally starts in the mind and manifests in the natural.

*"You have heard that it was said, you shall not commit adultery. But I say to you that everyone who so much as looks at a woman with evil desire for her has already committed adultery with her in his heart." Matthew 5:27-28 AMPC*

Moreover, the Lord made all our body parts with intentionality. Prophetically speaking, our sexual organs work as a key that fits in the perfect lock (our individuals' wives). If the key doesn't fit what God intended, then it is the wrong lock. What am I saying? When we go out of bounds with the purpose of God's design, we partake in sin and gross perversion. Contrary to popular belief, the marriage bed "can" be defiled with sexual corruption (immorality, perversion, abnormality, etc.). Understand that Satan has perverted everything God created, which includes sex. Satan has his versions of sexual practices which are immoral (sex outside of marriage and adultery) and perverted (sodomy, which involves anal or oral sex)! If you're married or single and you're imitating what you saw in the past or currently see in pornography, you are simply perpetuating a spirit of perversion. Selah! Let those with spiritual ears hear what the Spirit of the Lord is saying.

**Here are five areas of sexual immorality:**

- **Fornication** (1 Thessalonians 4:3-5, 1 Corinthians 6:18-20, 1 Corinthians 7:2)
- **Adultery** (Exodus 20:14, Hebrews 13:4, Proverbs 6:32, Matthew 5:27-28)
- **Homosexuality** (Leviticus 18:22, Genesis 19:1-11, 1 Corinthians 6:9-11, Leviticus 20:13
- **Incest** (Leviticus 18:6, 2 Samuel 13:1-19)
- **Prostitution** (Deuteronomy 23:18, 1 Corinthians 6:15-16, Galatians 5:19, 1 Thessalonians 4:3-4)

As men of God, it is time to address the hidden things impacting us spiritually, mentally, and physically. Satan loves for us to keep everything in the dark, while God loves for us to live in His marvelous light. It takes a man who wants to please the Lord to walk away from things that displease Him (no matter how good things feel to our flesh). But those who want the grace of God without having to obey Him will continue to live outside of His will until it's too late to repent. Single and married men, let us not mess up eternity with the Lord in exchange for a short period of sexual immorality, adultery, and perversion that will land us in the eternal (everlasting) lake of fire! We're in the last days, and Jesus is extremely soon to come.

# Spiritual Doors

Spiritual doors are one of the topics we don't hear much about in the body of Christ. However, it's a crucial topic that I must address. With biblical knowledge and understanding, we have the power to confront and close the spiritual doors we opened unknowingly. If ungodly spiritual doors remain open, demon spirits will continue to have legal access to our lives. Whether we're married or single, if we're engaging in any sexual sins, demonic doors (invisible doors in the spirit realm) are open in our lives. Sexual sins are not restricted to being sexually active with an individual but sexual sins also involve watching pornography and masturbating (as mentioned in the previous subject matter). Pornography and masturbation are sexual sins regardless if we're married or not. Ouch! Take a deep breath, fellas! I know it's a lot to take in because it challenges what we like (and our lust) versus God's intent.

Now that we've regained consciousness, we need to know that whatever spirit realm we evoke (stir up, arouse, trigger) will engage (join, take part, get involved) us in return. When demons see that we are doing things that please them and Satan, they come and partake. Darkness (sin) attracts darkness, and light (holiness) attracts light! As mentioned in the previous chapter, men of God still consistently engage in sexual immorality (married and single) because they haven't fully surrendered to the Lord. Where there is a lack of surrender to the Lord and from our sins, there are open doors in our lives (even when things seem to be going well). These spiritual open doors often cause us to deal with sexual dreams and sleep paralysis regularly. Sleep paralysis happens when a demon attacks us in our sleep. The demonic spirit prohibits our ability to move or speak for a certain amount of time. It's a horrible experience like no other! But it is caused by unrepentant sins, especially sexual sins. I dealt with sleep paralysis and demonic experiences for many years until I got completely serious in my walk with the Lord by fully living for Him. The demonic attacks by demons were so bad that I was afraid to sleep at night. Plus, I was going through these demonic occurrences as a saved man. My experiences prove that if we open our lives up to the demonic realm (through ungodliness, sexual immorality, witchcraft, etc.), demons have legal rights to be there! Demonic spirits attack us mostly at night because they love to hide and work in darkness. Evil spirits make demonic covenants with us in our dreams (the spirit realm) through sexual activity, eating, and even drinking. The demonic covenants we enter in our dreams affect our lives naturally until we break and renounce every evil covenant, repent, and walk in holiness. I will go into more detail below.

Nevertheless, my life changed once my relationship with God shifted to sold-out status. God delivered me from the demonic torture! The Lord opened my understanding to teachings and insight about spiritual warfare (vicariously through books, the Word, deliverance videos, and divine revelation), which taught me how to close spiritual doors and break the chains of the enemy off my life. My deliverance started with repentance (actual change) and renouncing the sins I used to engage in, which broke the covenants I made through sexual dreams and practices. For clarity and informational purposes, many evil covenants are made in our dreams when we're having sex with someone we know or don't know. However, if it's someone we know, it is not them but a demon spirit masquerading as them so that we can treat the dream as harmless instead of spiritual warfare hidden in disguise. In addition, eating and drinking in dreams represent us agreeing to an evil covenant with our name attached to it. Listen, the enemy uses what we love and what's familiar to us to bring us into bondage. When we sleep, we're in the realm of the spirit, which is when Satan and demonic spirits do their best work against us spiritually. Therefore, powerful warfare prayers (prayers that dismantle the works and plots of the enemy) are essential for us because they help us maintain our lives and free us from evil covenants. Prayer is one of our greatest safeguards against our enemies.

Countless saved men (and unsaved) worldwide are dealing with these same issues and more due to a lack of surrendering their spirit, soul, and body to Jesus. Double-mindedness keeps us bound and unstable in all our ways (see James 1:8)! In addition, many professed men of God live sexually immoral lives that surpass the sexual immorality of unbelievers. This statement of truth is shocking to many people but not to some. Why is that? Many Israelites (God's people) did the same thing! There is nothing new under the sun! However, it didn't end well for them. It's startling to know the number of Christians who believe it is impossible to live pure and holy lives. But it's more than possible through the Holy Spirit. The more we submit to the Lord (His Word) and His Spirit, the more liberated we become. The more we fall in Love with God, the more we fall out of love with sin. We can't get free from what we're unwilling to give up. Freedom requires a daily decision! Selah!

Moreover, the marriage bed is defiled in many marriages because husbands and wives have become indoctrinated by porn stars. In other words, couples are mimicking the sexual practices of individuals full of drugs and serving the devil. Anything that Satan has his influence on is defiled and perverted. Once more, all sexual practices are not of God. Satan's version of sexual practices doesn't align with God's original intent. Yahweh is intentional with His creations. But anything that creates confusion and perversion is from Satan. The more we know the Lord through His Word and intimacy (close relationship), the less we will argue and defend what He hates. Men are wondering why they're dealing with the spiritual things they're dealing with, and my answer is this, "spiritual doors are open that need to be closed immediately." I've made a list of important actions that are vital for our spiritual warfare tactics and lifestyle. These steps must be a part of our prayer life as often as needed because we are in a spiritual war that will continue until Jesus returns. Warfare is inevitable if we plan to fulfill God's kingdom purpose in the earth! However, we will fight effectively and win when we understand how to engage in spiritual warfare. Remember that we can't fight spiritual battles with ungodly doors open unless we plan to lose.

**Here are steps for self-deliverance and regular prayer points:**

1. Fast and Pray
2. Confess your sins to the Lord
3. Renounce every immoral practice you were involved in Jesus' name
4. Genuinely repent from all your sins (known and unknown)
5. Command every demonic spirit to come off and out of you in Jesus' name
6. Bind every familiar spirit (demonic spirit) that's operating in your life in Jesus' name and send them to the abyss to never return to the earthly realm again. *"And they begged [Jesus] not to command them to depart into the Abyss (bottomless pit)." Luke 8:31 AMPC*
7. Apply the blood of Jesus over yourself (spirit, soul, and body)

Sexual sins are extremely dangerous and will destroy our lives now and eternally. Sexual sins go beyond what I mentioned in this chapter, but the moral of this story is that all sins are open doors that give demons access to our lives. If we want to make it to Heaven, we can't live in unrepented sin. We can live righteous and holy lives, whether married or single if we want to! The Word and the Holy Spirit provide us with everything we need to please the Father. We have no excuses, but we do have a decision to make! Will we live clean lives with closed doors or dirty lives with open doors? Selah! Whatever we decide, we will eat the fruit thereof. Deuteronomy 30:15 says, *"See, I have set before you this day life and good, and death and evil."* Choose well by choosing God! Allow Jesus to deliver you from everything that is keeping you bound because He's willing and able to set you completely free. If you need help getting deliverance from evil spirits, seek help from someone who isn't afraid of the ministry of deliverance! You owe it to yourself! Freedom belongs to the people of God. The Word confirms that deliverance is the children's bread (see Matthew 15:22-28)!

One last thing, when we possess the Holy Spirit, we can't be possessed by demons. But we can be oppressed (disturbed, afflicted, weighed down, etc.) by them because of the spiritual doors we have open in the realm of the spirit. Demons are invisible spirits that can attach themselves to us and influence us to do wicked things based on our lust and desires. On the contrary, when a demon possesses an individual, it takes up residents in them as the Holy Spirit does with believers. Demonic oppression influences and demonic possession controls. This breakdown is the difference between being oppressed and possessed by demonic spirits. Since demons are disembodied spirits, they can hide in our body parts with an inability (unable, impossible, incapable) to possess us because we house the Holy Spirit. As born-again believers, we can be under the influence, impacted, oppressed, and diagnosed with issues caused by demonic spirits of infirmity, heaviness, fear, deception, lust, perversion, a lying spirit, etc. These evil spirits are proof that demons can oppress believers.

*"Shun immorality and all sexual looseness [flee from impurity in thought, word, or deed]. Any other sin which a man commits is one outside the body, but he who commits sexual immorality sins against his own body. Do you not know that your body is the temple (the very sanctuary) of the Holy Spirit Who lives within you, Whom you have received [as a Gift] from God? You are not your own, You were bought with a price [purchased with a preciousness and paid for, made His own]. So then, honor God and bring glory to Him in your body."* 1 Corinthians 6:18-20 AMPC

# CHAPTER NINE

# Stop Setting Yourself up to Fail!

When we want something really bad, we often make provision to get it even if it means overriding wisdom. Many of us place ourselves in compromising situations with the opposite sex, knowing we don't have the integrity to maintain a strong stance in the Lord, especially when she is what we want. Because of our negligence, we end up engaging in sexual sin due to a lack of accountability, self-control, and soundness of mind. As the Word says, we are led astray by our own hidden lust and desires.

*"Let no one say when he is tempted, I am tempted from God; for God is incapable of being tempted by [what is] evil and He Himself tempts no one. But every person is tempted when he is drawn away, enticed and baited by his own evil desire (lust, passions). Then the evil desire, when it has conceived, gives birth to sin, and sin, when it is fully matured, brings forth death." James 1:13-15 AMPC*

Kingdom men, we should never underestimate ourselves around a woman we're attracted to. We must always keep our spiritual guard up because the enemy knows what kind of women we like, and he'll make sure we are presented with our color and kind. It doesn't matter how anointed we are, everyone is subject to fall if we don't walk in God's Word, wisdom, and the Holy Spirit. Let's check out two powerful men (Solomon and Samson) from the Word who fell because of their disobedience to the Lord. They literally set themselves up for failure by yoking up with women who were out of covenant with Yahweh and in covenant with false gods.

*"Do not be unequally yoked with unbelievers [do not make mismated alliances with them or come under a different yoke with them, inconsistent with your faith]. For what partnership have right living and right standing with God with iniquity and lawlessness? Or how can light have fellowship with darkness? What harmony can there be between Christ and Belial [the devil]? Or what has a believer in common with an unbeliever?"2 Corinthians 6:14-15 AMPC*

### First example:

Before King David died, he instructed his son Solomon to keep the ways of God (because he was next in line to be king), His commandments, and precepts so that he may prosper in all he decides to do and everywhere he chooses to go. The Lord also warned Solomon about obeying all His commands, decrees, and regulations so his royal throne could be established over Israel forever. But if Solomon disobeys the Lord's instructions and turns from following Him, the fulfillment of God's promises concerning him will be forfeited due to disobedience.

After becoming King Solomon, he asked the Lord for wisdom to govern His people well (with justice) and to know the difference between right and wrong (discernment). Because Solomon asked for wisdom and not material possessions, long life, or the death of his enemies, the Lord gave Solomon great wisdom. In addition, God gave Solomon riches and fame (money, significant wealth, and massive influence), which he didn't ask for. Solomon intentionally represented God well and did amazing works on His behalf.

Now King Solomon loved many foreign women and married them as well. However, the Lord instructed the people of Israel (His people) not to marry foreign women because they would turn their hearts to false gods. But Solomon (the wisest man that ever lived) decided to override the wisdom of God. In Solomon's old age, the foreign women he loved so much influenced him to worship their false gods instead of remaining faithful to the one True God—Yahweh. Solomon went from being highly favored by the Lord to worshipping detestable gods. Solomon did what was evil in the sight of the Lord because he stopped following His and his father's instructions. The foreign women Solomon loved so much caused him to turn his heart away from Yahweh (the God of all creation) only to worship the false and detestable God Ashtoreth, Molech, and the gods of the Ammonites. As a result, Solomon's disobedience caused him to lose most of the kingdom, which hindered what his son had access to since he was next in line to be king. Idol worship will grossly affect our lives and bloodline. Solomon started right but ended up wrong due to surrendering his will to the influence of ungodly women. He set himself up for tremendous failure when he overrode God's wisdom and warning for the lust and desires of his carnal nature (see 1 King 3-11). Solomon was led astray by his own lust and evil desires.

## Second example:

An angel of the Lord instructed Samson's mother not to drink any alcoholic beverages nor eat any forbidden food. The angel also ordered Samson's parents never to cut his hair because they were to consecrate him to the Lord as a Nazarite. Samson not having his hair cut was a part of his Nazarite consecration that kept him in right standing with the Lord. Fast forward, Samson fell in love with Delilah (a woman who was out of covenant with God), a foreigner who was about to get paid for finding out where his strength comes from and how they could overpower and dismantle him (see Judges 16:6). Delilah hid men (the rulers of the Philistines) in a nearby room as a part of her plot against him. Samson gave her several ideas to challenge his strength, but none worked because he was undefeated! Despite many easy clues, Samson was not operating in sobriety (soberness) because he couldn't discern what Delilah was up to. He was so out of his mind because of her and the familiarity of his strength that he gave her several ways to trap him (see Judges 16:7-12). Samson set himself up to fail due to lust and being too familiar with winning. He didn't think he could lose because he always overpowered everything he encountered. Familiarity is a dangerous thing when we take it out of balance. We should never allow familiarity to become automation in our subconscious mind because we won't think about what we're doing or saying since our habits have become unconscious behavior. Selah!

Moreover, Delilah got frustrated and started manipulating Samson with her crying and nagging until he got irritated and revealed the secret of his power. Samson told Delilah, "My hair has not been cut!" He also admitted to Delilah that he was dedicated to God from birth as a Nazarite. After Samson revealed the power behind his strength, Delilah made him sleep with his head in her lap. She then called the men hiding in the other room to come in and cut off seven locks of his hair. Delilah awakens Samson to tell him the Philistines have come to capture him. However, he could not break free this time because he lost his strength. At this point, the Spirit of the Lord departed from Samson because his Nazarite vow was compromised (broken). Delilah got paid the promised money while the Philistines gouged out Samson's eyes. The Philistines took Samson to Gaza, where they shackled and imprisoned him. Samson could have avoided this situation by not connecting with a woman who didn't mean him any good. He had lots of strength and power but a lack of discernment and self-control (see Judges 16:15-22).

Men of God, just because we start right doesn't mean we will have a successful finish. If we want to live and finish according to God's intent, we must follow His instructions. One of the things that Solomon and Samson had in common was their love for women who served other gods. Secondly, they both set themselves up for failure due to a lack of wisdom and obedience to the Lord. A lack of honoring God and His instructions caused their life to end differently than intended. Here's an important question to meditate on: will you continue or place yourselves in a compromising situation manufactured to destroy you? Selah! I pray the answer is no! However, if you do or are currently in a position of such, know that sin (disobedience to the Lord) brings death and destruction. Hidden or known sins we refuse to correct will never give us a happy ending. The scripture above lets us know when sin fully matures; it brings forth death. Decide today that you will no longer set yourself up to fail but to win now and later by keeping the commands, precepts, and instructions of the Lord. Never underestimate the power of disobedience (sin).

# CHAPTER TEN

# Kingdom Men Versus Religious Men

We live in an age where people can't discern kingdom men of God from religious men who hold a form of godliness. Contrary to popular belief, both are not the same. In fact, we are either wheat or tear, godly or ungodly, kingdom-minded or carnally minded. A lack or an abundance of godly fruit (fruit of the Holy Spirit) will always determine who's tear and wheat. Kingdom men vary due to different maturity levels but are not tear. Some kingdom men are new in their walk (while others are more developed in the things of the Lord), but they are men submitted to God. In addition, kingdom men understand the kingdom mandate (or are being taught it) and maintain a relationship with the Father. Kingdom men are cultivated by uncompromising leadership that teaches the whole counsel of God's Word (with the demonstrations of the five-fold ministry). Lastly, kingdom men are no strangers to doing things according to the Word and pattern. Selah!

- *Therefore, you will fully know them by their fruits. Matthew 7:20 AMPC*

- *Let them grow together until the harvest; and at harvest time I will tell the reapers, first gather the weeds and tie them in bundles to be burned; but gather the wheat into my barn. Matthew 13:30 AMP*

## Kingdom Men

Kingdom men are ambassadors for Christ. That means we represent God on the earth. It also means we have the backing of Heaven as royal diplomats. In addition, kingdom men carry the heart and mind of Christ. We take the covenant of Jesus seriously because we are governed by the King of Glory (along with His Word and Spirit). Another thing we must know about kingdom men is that we are versatile. What do I mean? We understand how to operate in the systems of the world (whatever field of work God called us to reign in) as well as corporate worship assemblies. We are not confined to a religious building or mindset because we carry the Holy Spirit everywhere. In addition, we are living alters unto God, and he does not authorize us to turn off our belief system (like it's a light switch) at any time. Our belief is a lifestyle that represents the Kingdom of God. Our worldview is the very nature of the Lord because it is His Word. Our current world and all religions and denominations will no longer exist when Jesus returns. But the Kingdom of God (will remain the same), His standards, and the new earth and Heaven will fully manifest with all nations governed by the sovereign God–Yewhah! The ways of the Lord are everlasting (never changing). Therefore, kingdom people now live by the same moral standards already in Heaven. Kingdom men are God's royal priests and kings because we serve the King of kings, the Creator of everything! We are God's influencers in the systems of the world and the body of Christ.

Moreover, kingdom men love steak and potatoes (strong biblical food) because we understand we cannot live on cookies and cakes (motivational speeches ministering to our soul, not our spirit). God's kingdom ambassadors decree and declare and establish His will in the earth. Lastly, kingdom men are not associated with false gods, nor do we turn things and people into gods. However, if we are ignorant (lacking information) about an area where we have an unknown sin, we are quick to correct it as soon as we find out we're in error. We are about pleasing God over fleshly desires. The descriptions for kingdom men don't describe perfect men. There is no such thing! But it describes men who live holy, just, and righteous lives before the Lord. The life God requires of us is our reasonable service unto Him as His children. When we miss the mark (sin), we humble ourselves, repent, and continue living according to the Word of the Lord. The word of the Lord says, *"I beseech you therefore, brethren, by the mercies of God, that ye present your bodies a living sacrifice, holy, acceptable unto God, which is your reasonable service." Romans 12:1 KJV.*

**Before I give examples of religious men, let's read this prophetic definition and intent the Lord gave me about religion to set a foundation:**

First, we need to know that the Lord did not create religion, nor is He religious. Religion is Satan's suggestion and influence carried throughout the earth by man. Religion's influence causes us to prioritize human matters without considering God and His word. In other words, religion caters to the will of human desires without regard to God's divine will. Humanism is hidden in religion! Humanism is a way of life centered on the interest and values of humans without any respect for the Lord or His ways.

### Religious Men

Religious men are self-centered instead of God-centered. They prefer strange fire instead of the pure fire of the Holy Spirit. Religious men know the Word from the letter standpoint but don't know the Spirit of the letter. How do we know? Their interpretations of the letter are always off when the Spirit of God (the Holy Spirit) is always right. In essence, the Holy Spirit reveals the written Word accurately without confusion. Moreover, religious men read their Bibles to preach a sermon but not to know the Lord and develop intimacy with Him. They have the sound of the culture but not God's kingdom. Many pretend to be concerned about God's sheep when they refuse to teach them the truth (the fullness of God's Word) that can save their souls. Religious men teach and preach what keeps their flock happy and the seats filled but not the standards and warnings of the Lord. Religious men fight for abortions but not the glory of God! Selah! Spirit-filled worship unto the Lord (when Holy Spirit interrupts church programs to minister to God's people) is not allowed where religious men shepherd a flock, but self-centered performances are welcome and celebrated. Religious men take advantage of God's grace by living like and worse than unbelievers, believing they will receive the same benefits as the faithful without repentance (turning entirely from our sins). Religious men serve multiple gods but not the God of all gods. In addition, they are new-age practitioners who hold a form of godliness, but their spirituality is rooted in witchcraft.

**Here are a couple of scripture references:**

- *This know also, that in the last days perilous times shall come. For men shall be lovers of their own selves, covetous, boasters, proud, blasphemers, disobedient to parents, unthankful, unholy, without natural affection, trucebreakers, false accusers, incontinent, fierce, despisers of those that are good, having a form of godliness, but denying the power thereof: from such turn away. 2 Timothy 3:1-3, 5 KJV*

- *Not that we are sufficient of ourselves to think anything as of ourselves; but our sufficiency is of God; who also hath made us able ministers of the new testament; not of the letter, but of the spirit: for*

*the letter killeth, but the spirit giveth life.*
*2 Corinthians 3:5-6 KJV*

• *But cowards, unbelievers, the corrupt, murderers,*
  *the immoral, those who practice witchcraft, idol*
  *worshipers, and all liars—their fate is in the fiery*
  *lake of burning sulfur. This is the second death.*
  *Revelation 21:8 NLT*

Religious men love to remind us of our past and not our future. Satan does the same thing because he's the accuser of the brethren (see Revelation 12:10). Like father like son! Also, religious men love to be noticed by people they consider important. They absolutely love to be front and center to receive the glory and praise of the people when it all belongs to the Lord. Religious men judge what God hates as correct (they justify ungodly behavior) to keep themselves relevant and influential among many morally bankrupt people. In addition, they justify their right to do ungodly rituals that entangle and bind them to deities (demonic spirits) through spiritual covenants, oaths, and rituals. Religious men live immoral lives that contradict the life of godly disciples. They are oppressed by demonic spirits and in need of deliverance. However, religious men don't believe in the "Ministry of Deliverance" because they don't believe Christians can be oppressed by evil spirits, even though many professed believers (which includes ministry leaders) live sexually immoral lifestyles.

Moreover, religious men deny the truth written in the Word. They side with the world more than with the Word—Jesus! Sexual immorality, adultery, and perversion are consistently a part of their lifestyle. Religious men are gatekeepers because they only want themselves and those they approve of teaching and preaching the Word. These religious men prefer the rich to sit up front and the poor in the back. They are certified oppressors that betray people for worldly gain because money is their god. Religious men promote cultural influence over the Kingdom of God. Lastly, these men will stick with passed-down traditions and denominational beliefs rather than what's eternally written in the Word of the Lord.

**Here's a few scriptures of Jesus' response to the religious leaders of His time:**

- *Then Jesus said to the crowds and to his disciples, "The teachers of religious law and the Pharisees are the official interpreters of the law of Moses. So practice and obey whatever they tell you, but don't follow their example. For they don't practice what they teach. They crush people with unbearable religious demands and never lift a finger to ease the burden. "Everything they do is for show. On their arms they wear extra wide prayer boxes with Scripture verses inside, and they wear robes with extra long tassels. And they love to sit at the head table at banquets and in the seats of honor in the synagogues. They love to receive respectful greetings as they walk in the marketplaces, and to be called 'Rabbi. Matthew 23:1-7 NLT*

- *What sorrow awaits you teachers of religious law and you Pharisees. Hypocrites! For you shut the door of the Kingdom of Heaven in people's faces. You won't go in yourselves, and you don't let others enter either. "What sorrow awaits you teachers of religious law and you Pharisees. Hypocrites! For you cross land and sea to make one convert, and then you turn that person into twice the child of hell you yourselves are! Matthew 23:13, 15 NLT*

- *What sorrow awaits you teachers of religious law and you Pharisees. Hypocrites! For you are so careful to clean the outside of the cup and the dish, but inside you are filthy—full of greed and self-indulgence! You blind Pharisee! First wash the inside of the cup and the dish, and then the outside will become clean, too. "What sorrow awaits you teachers of religious law and you Pharisees. Hypocrites! For you are like whitewashed tombs— beautiful on the outside but filled on the inside with dead people's bones and all sorts of impurity. Outwardly you look like righteous people, but inwardly your hearts are filled with hypocrisy and lawlessness. Matthew 23:25-28 NLT*

After reading the scriptures above, it is safe to say Jesus hated religiosity! Religion keeps us from God's true nature and intent and out of His divine will. If we want to consistently grow in the Lord and be who He called us to be, we must live the Word, maintain an intimate relationship with Him, and refuse to be contaminated by the world. Lastly, religious men cheery pick the Word, but kingdom men eat the fullness of it! Now is a great time to decide if you are a kingdom man or a religious one. Choose well by choosing the Lord and all His ways.

*"I am the Vine; you are the branches. Whoever lives in Me and I in him bears much (abundant) fruit. However, apart from Me [cut off from vital union with Me] you can do nothing." John 15:5 AMPC*

# CHAPTER ELEVEN

# Generational Wealth & Divine Legacy

Generational wealth is one of the most important subjects in this book. To possess wealth is to have an abundance that ranks high in value beyond what is sufficient for one person, a family, a business, or a nation. The most significant wealth and legacy we can ever build and pass down our bloodline is the Word (Jesus) and how to worship and honor God. Many people discuss building wealth for their families, but the wealth they refer to is the lowest form, money. I'm not saying that money is unimportant because it is a vital necessity for living in the earth. However, knowing God through His Word plus intimately (a personal relationship) exceeds any form of monetary or material wealth. Proverbs 13:22 AMPC says, *"A good man leaves an inheritance [of moral stability and goodness] to his children's children, and the wealth of the sinner [finds its way eventually] into the hands of the righteous, for whom it was laid up."* If we live with abundant money and material blessings but die and lose our souls to Satan, what did we accomplish by having all we had? Absolutely nothing because we didn't have a good finish. The will of God is for no man to be lost but for humanity to be reconciled to Him (through Jesus) and not Satan. If we don't know and have the Father, the Son (Jesus), and the Holy Spirit, then we don't have true wealth, which means we're not passing the most important legacy to our children and beyond.

**Here are a few scriptures to consider and meditate on:**

- *For what does it profit a man to gain the whole world, and forfeit his life [in the eternal kingdom of God]? Mark 8:36 AMPC*

- *A good name [earned by honorable behavior, godly wisdom, moral courage, and personal integrity] is more desirable than great riches; And favor is better than silver and gold. Proverbs 22:1 AMP*

- *Praise the Lord! (Hallelujah!) Blessed (happy, fortunate, to be envied) is the man who fears (reveres and worships) the Lord, who delights greatly in His commandments. [Deut. 10:12.] His [spiritual] offspring shall be mighty upon earth; the generation of the upright shall be blessed. Prosperity and welfare are in his house, and his righteousness endures forever. Psalm 112:1-3 AMPC*

- *Do not gather and heap up and store up for yourselves treasures on earth, where moth and rust and worm consume and destroy, and where thieves break through and steal. But gather and heap up and store for yourselves treasures in heaven, where neither moth nor rust nor worm consume and destroy, and where thieves do not break through and steal; For where your treasure is, there will your heart be also. Matthew 6:19-21 AMPC*

God will never tell us to place money and material things above Him and His Word because man-made things are temporary treasures on the earth. However, divine treasures from God are eternally stored in Heaven and don't rust, rot, decay, or become outdated. In reference to our current and upcoming generations, we are under a fierce attack from Satan and his army of demonic spirits because they want us to chase things, people, money, false gods, and selfish ambitions. Why is that? Because these wrong motives go against God. Our enemies want us and our children to be out of alignment with the Lord and His Word because it hinders godly legacy and deliverance. One of the easiest ways the enemy ensures we are corrupt as a people is to have us replace divine wealth with earthy possessions (by any means necessary) that are losing value by the second compared to the wealth that comes from God. Many don't study the Word or have great teachers to teach and explain the Word (divine and eternal wealth), so we don't prioritize Jesus as our vital necessity. Since the Lord isn't a priority to many of us, we can't pass down a divine legacy to our kids or anyone else. We can't offer or teach what we don't have or know. Selah! This perpetuation (continuation) of not worshipping the Lord and studying His Word has birthed a generation only interested in material possessions but not the God of their salvation. Just know that Satan has the upper hand in our lives when we don't have a relationship with the Father (the kind that changes us into His nature). Hence why many of our hands are spiritually tied because we don't understand who we are and our authority in Jesus Christ. Righteousness (what the Lord calls right) exults individuals and nations to divine greatness, but sin brings down and destroys everything (see Proverbs 14:34).

*"Uprightness and right standing with God (moral and spiritual rectitude in every area and relation) elevate a nation, but sin is a reproach to any people."* **Proverbs 14:34 AMPC**

Having the wisdom of God (in every area of our lives) is essential because money and anything of value placed in the hands of a fool are detrimental. Money in the hands of people who don't know God will destroy them inwardly and outwardly now and eternally! In God's kingdom, He is our wealth and prosperity. Our position as kingdom men (and believers in general) is to seek God's kingdom and His righteousness first, and everything that's for us will be released to us (see Matthew 6:33) at His appointed time. The Lord doesn't have any problem with us having earthly wealth and riches. But He doesn't want us to place money and material possessions above Him. Solomon is the perfect example of an all-around wealthy and influential person who got what he had the righteous way. Solomon never asked for wealth, riches, or influence. However, God gave him all three because he asked for wisdom on governing His people and knowing the difference between good and evil (discernment). Solomon sought the Lord first, and the Lord gave him everything he needed and what he didn't ask for.

**Here's our passage of scriptures for confirmation:**

*"Solomon replied, "You showed great and faithful love to your servant my father, David, because he was honest and true and faithful to you. And you have continued to show this great and faithful love to him today by giving him a son to sit on his throne. "Now, O Lord my God, you have made me king instead of my father, David, but I am like a little child who doesn't know his way around. And here I am in the midst of your own chosen people, a nation so great and numerous they cannot be counted! Give me an understanding heart so that I can govern your people well and know the difference between right and wrong. For who by himself is able to govern this great people of yours?" The Lord was pleased that Solomon had asked for wisdom. So God replied, "Because you have asked for wisdom in governing my people with justice and have not asked for a long life or wealth or the death of your enemies— I will give you what you asked for! I will give you a wise and understanding heart such as no one else has had or ever will have! And I will also give you what you did not ask*

*for—riches and fame! No other king in all the world will be compared to you for the rest of your life!" 1 Kings 3:6-13 NLT*

Moreover, when God blesses us with wealth and riches, it's not merely for us to buy big houses, fancy cars, and name-brand clothing. The Lord loves nice things too! Heaven is luxurious! God gives us wealth and riches, so we can help advance His kingdom in the earth. We're supposed to build businesses that represent godly moral standards. As men of God (and believers in general), we're supposed to lend to many nations without having to borrow. In addition, God expects us to give to the poor and needy and help widows in need. If we only desire to build generational wealth so that we can live lavish lives and make our children rich, then we are operating from our agenda and not the heart and Word of God. The intent of the Lord always includes the needs and salvation of people and the demonstration of His kingdom. Remember, we never have to go to Satan to get anything because the Lord owns everything! In fact, God gives us power, wisdom, and witty inventions to achieve wealth and riches (see Deuteronomy 8:18). As men of God, we must get serious about our relationship with the Lord because Satan is serious about destroying us, our children, and our children's children. There is so much more to life than our insurance policies. Nevertheless, the only insurance policy that keeps us from missing Heaven is Jesus! Selah!

This teaching is a clarion call for men (and all believers) to advance God's kingdom by becoming who God called us to be. If we want to know and dismantle what is causing us to be out of God's will, we must abide in the most significant inheritance of all humanity, and His name is Jesus—The Word! Then we must take our priceless inheritance (Jesus) and pass Him to our children as the ultimate legacy and eternal (everlasting) wealth. It is our responsibility to ensure we are God's righteous people and not the wicked people of

Satan. If we're dishonest people with a lot of monetary and material wealth stored up, the Lord will see that it's transferred the His righteous people (those who faithfully worship Him full-time). It literally pays (in multiple ways) to be righteous people living within God's kingdom precepts and standards! Remember, true generational wealth and legacy are Yahweh, Jesus (the Word), and the Holy Spirit! These three are one! Things will seek us when we seek Him— the God of all Creation and everlasting wealth and riches.

# ARE YOU SAVED ?

# John 3:16

*"For God so [greatly] loved and dearly prized the world, that He [even] gave His [One and] [a]only begotten Son, so that whoever believes and trusts in Him [as Savior] shall not perish, but have eternal life. For God did not send the Son into the world to judge and condemn the world [that is, to initiate the final judgment of the world], but that the world might be saved through Him. Whoever believes and has decided to trust in Him [as personal Savior and Lord] is not judged [for this one, there is no judgment, no rejection, no condemnation]; but the one who does not believe [and has decided to reject Him as personal Savior and Lord] is judged already [that one has been convicted and sentenced], because [b]he has not believed and trusted in the name of the [One and] only begotten Son of God [the One who is truly unique, the only One of His kind, the One who alone can save him]. John 3:16 AMP*

# Prayer for Salvation and Reconnection

Father God, I love You. I need You. I want You in my life. I repent of all my sins (known and unknown), and I change my mind about those sins to take on the Mind of Christ. God, I denounce and renounce any idol gods, I've ever placed before You and any idol gods, I've come into a covenant agreement with outside of You.

I surrender to You, God, as my Father and receive Jesus as my Savior and Lord. I believe He died for the world's sins, including mine, and rose from the dead on the third day. God, I invite Your Holy Spirit to come in and take up residence within me and to be filled by Him. Father, I receive You right now, and at this very moment, I believe with my whole heart that You've heard my prayer and that I am now saved (old things have passed away, and all things have become brand new) in Jesus' name, Amen!

Get planted in a church that teaches and operates from a kingdom perspective, not man-made rules and traditions. God's original intent is for the body of Christ to become mature, perfected, and fully equipped by the whole counsel of His Word, which can only come through the five-fold ministry (see Ephesians 4:11-13). That's God's intent and order!

# About The Author

**Michael Moorer** has committed his life to serving God and humankind. A pioneer of destiny, Mr. Moorer is a man of worship who operates with high moral standards. He is also a creative mentor, entrepreneur, and author of several books, among many other talents. Michael Moorer has also gained domestic and international influence through his prolific literary work. God's calling on Michael's life is further solidified in his career, aiding other creatives and those who are broken, lost, depressed, or may wrestle with an identity crisis. Mr. Moorer is the perfect candidate to minister to the soul of those who struggles in the areas previously mentioned because the Lord delivered him from those same strongholds and more. By faith in God, the Creator of the universe, Michael Moorer, provides prophetic insight and revelation with a clear message of truth, hope, reformation, deliverance, and restoration through the Love of Jesus Christ. With Michael's drive and love for the Lord, there is no doubt that the Most High God favors him!

Made in the USA
Columbia, SC
23 June 2023

18844610R00052